Real People
Real Lives

Volume Two

CW01067104

By
Michelle Welch

Illustrations by Kevin McKenzie

Light News Publishing, Manchester, England
www.lightnewspublishing.co.uk

Real People Real Lives

Volume Two

By
Michelle Welch

Illustrations by Kevin McKenzie

Light News Publishing
PO Box 93, Manchester
M16 7BQ
England

website: www.lightnewspublishing.co.uk
e-mail: info@lightnewspublishing.co.uk

First Published 2008

British Library Cataloguing in Publication Data

A catalogue record of this book is available from the British Library.

ISBN1-870645-09-10

Cover Design, Typesetting, Printing and Production by:

Agape Press (UK) Limited
www.agapepress.co.uk

Dedication

To two most amazing people:

Michael Brown whose story
I have not yet been able to tell,
but the day is almost here.

Davinia Smith you are
a young woman of courage,
an overcomer and
a woman of victory.

Contents   Page

Acknowledgements

I am eternally grateful to:

Don Okpalugo of Agape Press. Not only are you the man who prints my books but you have taught me all of the processes involved in putting together a book, from the initial idea in the mind, to getting the finished product on a bookshelf. You have also inspired me to follow the dream and to trust that God will bring to pass that which he has revealed.

Kevin McKenzie. You have partnered me in the vision of Real People Real Lives and people have been moved as much by your illustrations as with the words of the texts.

Debbie Marshall. You spent your holiday proof reading my manuscript and gave me valuable and objective feedback especially in regard to finding my own writing style. Hopefully you will see that I have taken it on board.

Preface

Today I am faced with an irony. On TV I am watching the interview of a mother whose life has been tragically changed by the murder of her fifteen year old son. He was a black boy who it would seem had the whole world ahead of him. At the same time, I am led to consider the hundreds of men and women whom I have met in our prisons. Some have committed minor and petty offences whilst others have committed some of the most atrocious crimes that one can even imagine. Is it possible to appreciate the pain of those who are said to be the victims, whilst at the same time comprehend the lives of those who might be said to have caused their suffering? In trying to answer this question, I have come to the conclusion that we are all victims to some extent. By this I mean that we are all victims to suffering. The physical life of a man is a journey with a beginning and ultimately an end. Suffering creates victims and every human being at some stage of their journey must and will come face to face with suffering. This begs the age old philosophical question, 'If there is a God, why does he allow suffering?' In the pages of this book and in the stories of the men and women who share their experiences of suffering, I think that you will find an answer.

Real People Real Lives Volume Two follows the pattern of its predecessor, Real People Real Lives. I am a story teller, not one who tells the stories of fictional characters, but of real people. This book is a compendium of stories from ordinary people who have faced some real life issues. Throughout my life I have met some amazing people who have suffered from adversity. In fact I live my life believing that I am in a privileged position having met the people that I have along my own journey of life. I am truly touched with compassion as I deliver each story that has been shared with me. Each one has strengthened me to believe that despite the difficulties that life throws in our faces we do not have to remain victims, but can finish victorious. Life brings choices and we can either choose to let our circumstances depress us so that we retain the mentality of a victim, or we can choose to rise above our circumstances and be victorious. Even though some of the stories may sadden you, I believe that the people in this book fall into the second category, they are victors. Each of them has at some time called upon God and can testify that it is the love of God which has enabled them to come through their trials and tribulations. Their stories are accounts of victory and hope.

Real People Real Lives Volume Two has not been written as an academic book but has been designed so that it is easy to read. In fact it has been made as simple as possible to enable it to reach even those who would not usually pick up a book to read. I believe that it will give you the reader a hope for your future knowing that the Lord God can, will and does come into our lives and carries us through adversity. If you are a victim then it is not too late; you too can become victorious!

Michelle Welch February, 2008

Chapter 1

War

As I ran from the militia, I hid behind a bush and it was from there that I watched as they hacked my father, two sisters and brother to death.

> *For I have learned in whatever state I am to be content;*
> *I know how to be abased, and I know how to abound.*
> *Everywhere and in all things*
> *I have learned to be full and to be hungry,*
> *Both to abound and suffer need.*
> *I can do all things through Christ who strengthens me.*
>
> *Philippians 4:11-13*

I was born into a very poor background in Rwanda in East Africa. My mum who was separated from my dad was actually from Uganda whilst my dad was Rwandese of the Tutsi tribe. At times things were so hard that we found it a struggle to eat and I remember that it was not uncommon for us to live on handouts. Because of their separation I found myself living between both parents and although they struggled, I was able to go to school and attain O' and A' Levels. However, due to the lack of money, I was not able to go to university, but instead I obtained some secretarial qualifications and I also completed some computer courses.

During 1993, I worked for a brief spell in Uganda, and then in early 1994 I went to Rwanda where I joined my siblings and my dad. Four months after returning to my father's home, the bloody civil war broke out. It was a sunny day in April 1994 that the catastrophe reached us, and the militia eventually came to our home. I remember my dad trying to bribe them, offering them money in exchange for our lives. But as history shows, this war was not about money, it was about the extermination of human life and the genocide of a people. It was then that I made a decision that was to drastically alter my life. People were running past our house and as a young person facing danger, I instinctively joined them. However, the other members of my family remained behind. As I ran from the militia, I hid behind a bush and it was from there that I watched as they hacked my father, two sisters and brother to death. In desperation I tried to run back to them but a neighbour held on to me.

How I felt is indescribable and the guilt that I carry around for their deaths is unbearable. To this day I feel that I never did enough; maybe I could have done more to prevent what had happened. But of course I know that it was impossible to do anything that would have kept them alive, but the guilt that I hold never fades. In fact it's been eleven years since that terrible day but it still feels like yesterday. There are times when I fall asleep and dream back to the happy times and then suddenly I am confronted with the horrific ordeal. At other times it's as if I am watching a movie and as though I'm watching someone else's life, not my own.

From that moment I was on my own and to survive I had to spend my time running and hiding. I would hide anywhere, in churches, hospitals, convents, in the bush and there were even times when I had to lie amongst dead bodies to pretend that I was dead. But I miraculously survived and finally made it to my mom's home in Uganda. She had been told that we had all been slaughtered so when she saw me she fainted.

During my time on the run, even though I had been brought up in a strict Christian household, I doubted the existence of God. I found it a struggle to fathom how a loving, kind and caring Father in heaven would allow one million people to be slaughtered like animals in a matter of one hundred days. Whilst I was on the run and hiding in various churches I found that they were not the safe houses that they were intended to be and in fact it was some of the leaders of the church, the so called men of God, who were the ones who would initiate and organise the murders. Nothing made sense. What could I do but question God?

As time went by I tried to put the past behind me. I began to rebuild my life in Uganda and found work. Sometime in 1997 I decided to go back to Rwanda as the war was over and I felt a need to return to search for any surviving relatives. I returned to Rwanda, but whilst on my way out of the country I was arrested on allegations of spying. I tried convincing the people who had me arrested that I wouldn't spy on my own country as I was one of theirs, but my pleas fell on deaf ears. The problem was that I could not identify myself as any trace of identification that I'd possessed had been destroyed during the war. You see it was from our identity cards that one could prove which tribe we came from, and it was this information that would lead to us being massacred. However, after two weeks of horrendous torture, I was released pending investigations.

On my release I left the country and returned to Uganda but trouble seemed to follow me and again I was arrested by officials. They had received allegations that several people were spying on the country and they had reason to believe that I was one of them. Similarly to my previous arrest, I had to endure torture, interrogations and things that I can't even mention. After a period of two weeks I was released. I was innocent and it was this fact that kept me going. Nevertheless, five years later I was re-arrested by the same people. This to me was a sign showing me that I needed to sort out my life. I was tempting fate and it was time for a change.

In 2002 I started planning to leave the country and some friends introduced me to someone who would be able to get me out. Since I did not have any money, the guy convinced me that it would be possible to repay him in a short period of time on arrival at our destination. In July 2003 I therefore embarked on a journey to the 'Promised Land'. Arriving in London, England, an alien country to me and having no one to lean on but the guy who had brought me, I had no choice but to go with him to his place of residence. I was convinced that things would sort themselves out. By the third day I was still in his flat and it was on that night that my terrible nightmare began. I was raped three times and this became a daily ordeal for me for a period of a year when I would be raped by my host and his colleagues. At one time I thought that the only thing that would save me would be death but even that wasn't forthcoming. Some of the men who were raping me looked unwell and after some months I begged my host to see a doctor. It was then that my host revealed to me that he was HIV positive. I then went ahead and had tests which proved what I had feared all along. After being abused for several months I was almost developing AIDS so I was started on medication immediately.

Imagine, here I was in a strange country with no friends or family and no form of identification. I depended on my host, a psycho-maniac, who would threaten me day in and day out. In fact one day I tried to escape but he found me. The punishment that I received for my failed escape was severe. I needed to get away from his so I decided to use a different approach and had 'peace talks' with him. This approach worked and eventually he came round to my point of view and he released me. Because of the business that he was involved in, he easily processed a counterfeit passport for me and coached me on how to go about working and living in the UK. Then he let me go. I had escaped from his clutches and so I travelled to Manchester where I started hunting for jobs. I applied for a National Insurance number with my fake passport. I knew that it was a fake but out of desperation and having suffered at the hands of those men, I guess I would have done anything. All I had ever wanted was to be able to get shelter, food and clothing. I had not been aware of any benefit entitlements that might be made available with having a National Insurance number and it was not these that I was seeking. Nonetheless, as I went to pick up my passport from the Job Centre I was arrested. My punishment was imprisonment for eight months but then I was finally released.

That's me so far. I have applied for asylum and so far all of my appeals have been rejected and I'm now in an immigration detention centre. I know for a fact that if I am sent back to Rwanda or Uganda I will end up dying within twelve months either from prison torture or worse still, from lack of HIV medication. I am a human being and can only do so much. I've tried to do what I can do myself but now I have decided to let God take over. My faith in God has been restored and I have no-one but him to trust in. The one thing I've vowed to God is that if I am allowed to remain in England, I plan to spend the few years that I have left, working in his service. My health is deteriorating and I don't know how long I will live but as it is God who gives life and takes life, I have to give special praise for everyday that I am alive. When I consider where I have been and what I have gone through, I know it's because of his will that I am here now and my prayer to him is 'Lord, let your will be done.'

Chapter 2

Cancer - Death

During the surgery her body was opened up and found to be riddled with cancer.

> *Do not lay up for yourselves treasures on earth,*
> *Where moth and rust destroy*
> *And where thieves break in and steal;*
> *But lay up for yourselves treasures on earth,*
> *Where neither moth nor rust destroy*
> *And where thieves do not break in and steal.*
> *For where your treasure is, there your heart will be also.*

Matthew 6:19-21

My mum died in April 1998 after suffering from cancer. She had spent all of her life working hard. Migrating from Jamaica to England in the early 1960's, she had never wanted to buy a home in England, instead it was always her dream to purchase a house in her native land for her retirement. Her dream was fulfilled when she bought a property for $250,000 Jamaican dollars, to which all of the family had contributed. Years before she passed away, I remember my mum travelling to Jamaica and measuring up for the curtains for her new home. I was her eldest daughter in England and also the seamstress of the family so I made her some beautiful drapes which were bright yellow reflecting the Jamaican sun. She also bought all that she needed; the net curtains, the furniture, beds, microwave and other household items in preparation for her return.

At the time that my mum retired, my dad was very ill and in fact I always thought that he would die before her. She began to prepare for her retirement in Jamaica, packing her barrels with all that she would require. However in April 1997, she began to feel unwell in her body. She had left it a couple of months before going to the doctors, thinking that she had no more than constipation. But when her stomach began to swell, I encouraged her to go for a check up. She was given some tablets and apart from the swelling, continued to live and to walk around as normal.

Her GP referred her to the local hospital for further tests and after her visit I remember her coming home crying, 'I'm going to die, I've got cancer.' I tried to reassure her that she would be alright; after all there was a cure for cancer, I thought. We prayed. I was so glad that she was a Christian. Ten years earlier, things were different, she wasn't a Christian serving God out of love, but someone who served God out of obligation.

After further tests, my mum was referred to a cancer specialist hospital in Manchester. She had been told that if an operation was performed she could be saved, but what man thinks and what God knows are sometimes two different things. During the surgery her body was opened up and found to be riddled with cancer; in fact it was likely that she'd had it for some years. We realised that she would not get better and she was given six months to live. It was hard on my dad; he was going to lose his soul mate. But in my heart I wished it was him instead of my mum as our relationship had not been close. On April 11th 1998 at 11.40pm my mum died. I personally was angry with God.

My mum had remained a cheerful person throughout it all. As people came to visit her she would be the one who strengthened and encouraged them. She would tell them not to cry if they were coming to see her and she had a joy and a peace because she knew where she was going. She wasn't afraid of death. It was a time that I was suffering from an illness myself, a thyroid problem which was being dealt with by steroids. My younger sister was living in Australia with her boyfriend so came back, whilst my older sister had travelled from Jamaica. Mum had not wanted to die in a hospital so had come home.

I remember vividly the day that she died, all of the family was there along with the priest. It was Easter Saturday so I had saved a chocolate cream egg for her to eat but she didn't make it to Easter Sunday. Normally I would go home at around 10pm in the evenings but for some reason, I decided to stay that night with my mum. She was in pain and I phoned the doctor but he said that there was nothing that could be done. My dad didn't know what to do. I phoned my other family members to come. I watched her die. To know that I saw my mum take her last breath strengthens me, 'Wow!' I cried on the day that she died but have never cried over her since.

The funeral arrangements were made; I made her dress and her wreath. The cemetery part of the funeral was hard as I knew that she was not there. At the graveyard, I kept a distance as I didn't want to watch her being put into the ground. Even to this day it's as though my mum's just gone away on holiday to Jamaica. I haven't come to terms with the cemetery bit and don't know if I ever will. I've never been to a cemetery since even though I have been to a number of funerals, as I still think that they are cold and horrible places. My brothers go to visit her grave to talk to her but as the only Christian member of the family I know that she is with God and not in the grave.

My mum's death was not in vain. As a result of her passing away my dad and I have become closer and I have got to know him better. After my mum's death, I didn't want to speak to him and I wished it had been him who had died. I used to hate him and felt that he was an abuser, but my mum had specifically asked me to look after him as we would be the only family that he had left. I thank God, I have been able to forgive him and the pain and the bad feelings have gone and we are now the best of friends. I'm glad that it wasn't him who had died as he would have died with me hating him.

The key thing that I have learnt from my mum's death is that it is important not to concentrate on storing up our riches on this earth. The most important thing that we can do is to do what God wants us to do and that is to obedient to be his will. If we do this we are actually storing up riches in heaven which are not perishable and cannot be destroyed. My mum had a plan to return to Jamaica to her nice home which she had worked all of her life for, but the most important home that she was preparing was that in heaven where she would be reunited with the Father and his son Jesus. That is the greatest treasure that we can ever find.

Chapter 3

Murder, Twice!

Most things I just can't remember because at the time it was like a dream that I wanted to escape from.

> *The Lord is my shepherd*
> *I shall not want.*
> *He makes me to lie down in green pastures;*
> *He leads me besides the still waters.*
> *He restores my soul;*
> *He leads me in the paths of righteousness*
> *For his name's sake.*

Psalm 23:1-3

For He knows our frame;
He remembers that we are dust.
As for man, his days are like grass;
As a flower of the field, so he flourishes.
For the wind passes over it, and it is gone,
And its place remembers it no more.

Psalm 103: 14-16

In 1997 life was good and I was in a steady relationship, studying at university. Family life was good too, even though I hadn't spoken to my brother Kevin for nearly a whole year because he had wronged me. I felt that I couldn't forgive him and I refused to give in even though I missed him. I had to protect myself from it ever happening again. He had to learn that I was serious and that I would not stand for his behaviour any more.

I was out on the town with friends. I never felt the tug in my heart that you would expect to feel when someone you love dies. It was in the early hours of the morning and I received a phone call from a friend that I was to go home as something had happened to my brother Kevin. He had been shot twice before and had survived so what could this news be? He appeared to be invincible! On approaching the house I could see that it was serious because of the amount of people present. Cars were parked outside and in my heart I knew that he was dead. I went straight inside and asked my mum if it was true. She replied, 'Yes'.

The rest was a blur. I don't remember how I got through it, I just blanked it out. I didn't want to know or hear anything about it and I didn't want to see his body. I just stayed in my room and ignored everything that was going on. The house was always so busy with people that cared but couldn't comfort my grief and regret. IF ONLY! Why was I so stubborn? Why didn't I just forgive him? I hadn't spoken to him for a year, I had wanted to speak to him but I let pride get in the way. Unforgiveness had robbed me of the opportunity of being able to say, 'I love you.' I lost the chance and would never be able to get it back. I found it most easy to hide this unwanted reality with alcohol, but it always brought out my deepest feelings and anger. Guilt was consuming me on the inside - IF ONLY!

When the time of the funeral came I had to face it, I had to. It was a sunny day and friends and family were arriving at the house along with wreaths and flowers. Most things I just can't remember because at the time it was like a dream that I wanted to escape from. By the time his body arrived at the house, the fact that he was dead was beginning to kick in but I couldn't put his face to the corpse, so I stayed outside until it was his time to go.

I totally cut myself out of the preparation for the funeral. I couldn't handle it. Anyway my brother Dennis took care of most of it. I didn't even know the real story behind his murder. You know, I never knew I could cry so much. The church was packed with people. We had to sit right on the front row with the coffin in front of us. Even when the coffin went down into the grave I couldn't accept that it was my brother; I could not picture Kevin's face inside that box going six feet underground. I just held my mother tightly. I couldn't even face the reception. I couldn't face the people so I stood outside. I was so self-ish; I never considered my mum, whether or not she needed me. I just stayed away. This was an unwanted reality forcing itself upon me.

After the funeral everyone began to get back to their normal lives. The house was empty and quiet as there was now only myself, mum and my sister at home. Mum began to attend church on a regular basis and I occasionally went along with her too. Life went on. I continued to go to university. I had a boyfriend. I believed in God but was not a Christian and wasn't prepared to take it that far. My thinking was different and I had so many questions. If he was not a Christian, was my brother now condemned to hell? Kevin had been shot twice before but he was not invincible. I couldn't accept the reality of never ever seeing his face again. If only I'd said this or done that, maybe things might have been different.

It was extremely hard having to deal with the grief, with the illuminating family issues and family break up and with the back stabbing that ensued. People were saying things about him that were hurtful and irrelevant. I don't know how I got through it all, although I did lean heavily upon my boyfriend. When I look back I know that God was knocking on the door to my heart. While sitting on the fence and toying with the truth of God, a Christian friend of mine phoned me in the midst of her mental illness to tell me that I couldn't compromise the love of God. Even though this statement was in the midst of many others that did not make sense, it hit me hard. I couldn't reply because I knew it was the truth. All I could do was cry. She wasn't well, I knew that. What did she know anyway? What did she know about my life? Nothing, I thought but her statement was so the TRUTH. I just broke down and at first I couldn't tell anyone because I didn't know what to do. I confessed to know and love God even though my life remained the same.

One of my greatest fears was that of losing my boyfriend, my world. I knew that my lifestyle was unacceptable to God, but it was mine. I knew that it was wrong but again I ignored my conscience and got on with it. Change at that time was unthinkable. But God was faithful and remained with me. Even in my deepest sin, he was there. I continued to walk that road and life was up and down for the next three years. Then one day, history repeated itself and death came knocking - AGAIN!

It was 2000 and I was in the last week of my degree, the pressure was on and I was stressing out trying to get everything finished. Could it be possible? NOT DENNIS? I returned home from town and was studying in my bedroom when a friend of my brother knocked on the door asking for Dennis. He was quite concerned. I didn't think anything of it until we discovered that he was nowhere to be found. I phoned my other brother Tony and he told me that something was wrong, but forbade me to tell our mother. He instructed me to wait for him to call me back; at that point my heart began to leap and pound, so many questions. Where was Dennis now? What had happened to him? I began to pace the room too and fro. My mind was racing with many thoughts. Was he alive? Was he dead? Had he been kidnapped? Where was he? This just could not be happening again, but it was, it really was! I began to pray, I began to plead, and I began to bargain with God. 'Let him be okay, I don't care about my degree, I'll fail but just let him be alive.'

All sorts of things were coming up. How long was I going to have to wait? I just stayed in my room; how could I face my mum downstairs when I knew that something was wrong? Time seemed to drag on forever and ever. I phoned Tony back but there was no news. Later, he called me to say that he was coming round to the house. I had to wait a little longer. Then the car pulled up. I shot downstairs to meet my other brother Glen. Tony remained in the car. I could see it on their faces. HE WAS DEAD! Did I hear it right? Yes, he was dead, even though no one said a word. When I asked, it was confirmed. He was gone. He had been murdered on the Sunday and his body had been found the following morning in the nearby city of Leeds.

Once again the house became full of people. My life was taking a turn. I had a degree to complete and present but that was no longer important. What had been my main priority was now irrelevant. This had pushed me off the edge. The devil was really revealing himself to me. Where was God? Evil was present and very real to me. There must be a God. I began to humble myself; I no longer had all of the answers. I was hurt, broken and in shock, afraid of life, confused and angry. I was beginning to draw closer to God.

When the time came to view Dennis's body, I didn't have the courage to go into the room, so I just walked past the door. I remember seeing something on the table but one thing I knew for sure was that it wasn't my brother. What I saw changed my life and brought many questions. If that was not Dennis, who was it? It didn't even look like him. Is it possible that it could be him? I don't know what it was, but it wasn't my brother. I remember Dennis, his face, his smile and that was not him. But where was he? All of these questions. What made him smile? What made him speak? How could he be here one day and gone the next? What made him breathe? What made him move? What made Dennis Dennis? He was more than what I just saw on that table. Where had my brother gone?

God was with me in these times and he gave me comfort and kept me sane even though at times I thought I was going crazy. I began to understand that there was more to life than I could see and understand. We were more than just flesh. Dennis was more than just his decaying body. We had something on the inside. More questions needed more answers. How do we live? Why are we here? Who created us? I wanted answers. There had to be more to life than this, than what I could see. Why were we born? Was it to live a life just to die? I realised that I was no longer in control of my life, it wasn't my decision if I lived or died, the decision was made by a greater power. Dennis wanted to live but his life was taken away. The more I pondered on these things the more I understood that there was something bigger out there, God was real. I wanted to know more. I wanted to know the truth.

I was sick of my life, running around trying to be someone else, never satisfied. Was life really about killing and overworking myself to earn money to buy clothes to look good on the outside? It was pointless. All of it no longer made sense. I had someone on the inside. There was a person on the outside, ME, but who was the real person on the inside? This was important, I needed to know. I was more than flesh that dies and decays, I had a spirit.

I made up my mind to research all religions in order to find the truth and my way to God, I never got past the Bible. I understood that there was a spiritual world. I have always believed in God and known about Jesus, but he was never real to me. My family are all none Christians apart from my mum. I began to read a devotional booklet called the 'Word for Today', and that set me on track. I started to attend church more often. I was still seeing my boyfriend and at the same time walking closer and closer to God, but the closer I became the more things started to fall away. There was a change beginning in me, my personality, my attitude and my conscience.

As we went through the court trial of those accused of murdering Dennis, I had a peace and felt as though I was finding rest in the Lord. I prayed for justice but deep down in my heart, I felt that I didn't really care if we won the case. I had a comforter and a strong tower and my hate for those involved in the crime turned to pity. I could see the bigger picture even though the verdict against them was 'Not Guilty'. My mum broke down but I knew that God knows all things and that it would be alright, they would one day have to stand before him. I couldn't understand how people could be so evil. I had pity for the family and went up to them at the end of the trial to speak to them. There was no need for their behaviour but maybe they had no understanding.

My relationship with my boyfriend finally ended, unable to withstand the pressure. The Lord carried me all the way through with a peace that surpassed all understanding. My life changed and I began to commit myself to going to church on a regular basis. The word came alive and it felt like God was directly speaking to me through the pastor every Sunday as I sat in the congregation. I had been seeking for something but could never get the satisfaction that I needed. When the altar call was made one Sunday for salvation, I dropped my fears of change and gave my life to Jesus. I had fallen in love with God, my comforter and healer. I was totally free, no hindrances, He was the only thing that made sense. The decision was right and so was the time.

There have been times in my life when I never thought that I would smile again but now I can. My decision to follow Jesus is the best that I have made. I often wonder looking back, how I lived without knowing him, and having him to turn to and to lean upon. I thought I was in control of my own life. I wanted to know the truth, but I wasn't prepared to allow the truth to change my lifestyle. I'd always known the truth in my mind but not in my heart. I was good at covering things up, especially sin. I used statements like, 'I'm a good person', 'It's human nature', 'I'm only human,' and 'everyone does it.' I even changed the Lords prayer to suit me, omitting the parts about forgiveness. How could I forgive murderers? But forgiveness is a harsh truth and a necessary reality.

During this period, I realised that I wasn't in control of my own life and I wasn't promised tomorrow. We have to live life while we are still here, because one day our life will pass away on earth. This is a truth that I didn't think about and took for granted. But some things are true whether we want to believe them or not. Truth hurts and when I was faced with it, I was forced to step back in order to come forward.

Jesus is real and living. To follow Christ is not about change. I opened my heart to know the truth and he came in. God knows the desires of our hearts and the more intimate we become with him, the more he changes us, not by force but by love. I cannot tell you when the change took place, but the old habits began to fall away and things around me began to change. The more I read the bible, the more I began to look at life differently. I was just living life as normal but friends could notice the change in my character. As circumstances in my life changed, it wasn't an easy time, but Jesus kept me strong. In every storm there is a blessing and it was in the midst of a storm that I found Jesus, my friend and saviour.

I have never looked back or regretted my decision to follow Christ. It was the best thing that I have ever done and has changed my life and given me hope. My love for Christ and my hunger to know him through the bible has sent me to study at Bible School for two years. Also my search for more has taken me out of Manchester and opened my eyes to the world and the lost, people without a relationship with Jesus. Jesus is real! I've never seen him, but there have been times in my life when he has been more real to me than the people around me. I have found a resting place in the word of God that I know that he is real. The word is living and has touched and comforted me so many times when no one else could. One thing that I desire is that Jesus is lifted high and that people will step into his rest. No matter what you the reader may be going through, I want you to know that there is a way out with him. There was a way out for me. I was set free and the same opportunity is offered to you to.

Chapter 4

Witness

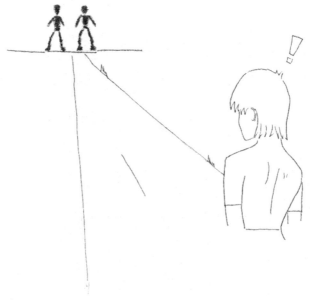

I didn't see the guys pass by but then it came, the sound of gunshot, I think I counted four.

> *'Whenever I am afraid,*
> *I will trust in You.*
> *In God (I will praise His word),*
> *In God I have put my trust;*
> *I will not fear.*
> *What can flesh do to me?'*

Psalm 56:3-4

It was July 2003 and a hot sunny evening on a quiet lane in an area of Clarendon, Jamaica. I was relaxing on the veranda with my sister and two other guys chatting about this and that. We had no worries, life was cool and we were chilling. I looked up and saw two men walking up the lane towards the house. Something seemed odd; these men were walking too fast. This was a Sunday evening and it was the time of day that people strolled. Work was out, there was no reason for people to rush today; it was the day that we released our stress and tension, a day to be laid back and to relax. Before the men reached the house I heard a voice say, 'Get up.' I obeyed. I don't know why? This was not a human voice but a voice in my head. My sister and the two other guys remained sitting. Did she not hear it? I went into the house, but again the voice in my mind told me to go further into the house. Why? I don't know but I moved. As I moved I glanced through the window to see if the two men were passing, they should have reached the house by now. I stood up and suddenly felt as though something was going to happen. I didn't see the guys pass by but then it came, the sound of gunshot, I think I counted four.

My sister reacted by jumping up and running and as she did one of our friends followed behind her. She ran into the road to stop a car not even knowing if it belonged to the gunmen. It wasn't but one of the gunmen did stop her and the friend and held them up, telling them not to move. It didn't stop there. The other one of our friends on the veranda was hit by a bullet which lodged into his spine. The gunmen disappeared as quickly as they had arrived leaving me, my sister and one of the guys unharmed. However our other friend was left crippled.

The irony of this shooting was that the friend who was shot didn't want me to act as a witness for the police, we were all witnesses to the crime that day but it seemed that our testimonies were of no importance. This shooting had been a targeted hit and the guy who had been shot was the target. He knew who the attempted assassins were. This was not a shooting that was going to be settled in the courts of law and by the police; the victim of the shooting was going to take the law into his own hands. The tables were to be turned and I was to be his first victim. Why? I was accused by him of being involved in setting him up. The reason he gave was that I had moved before the perpetrators approached them on the veranda so I therefore must have been aware and party to their plans. In his mind, I must have been involved. I was now a wanted person. He twice sent men to my home. On the first occasion I arrived home fifteen minutes after they had come and gone. The second time was an even closer shave; I arrived home five minutes after they had left. On this occasion my sister was at home. She saw the men but she hid and thankfully they didn't see her.

I was the wanted party and because of that I had to flee. My family is not a wealthy one and things sometimes are hard for us so I had to leave without any help or support from them. I know that I was under God's protection on that day. It was his voice that told me to get up. Maybe if I hadn't have got up at that moment, I might have been shot dead myself, after all I was sitting right next to the guy who took the bullets. Eighteen months later I'm still on the run and it is probably likely that they are still looking for me. However, though I am on the run, I have occasionally gone back home to see my mum. Yes, I have fear but I have to fight it and by the time I get to the house, it has usually totally gone. I still hear two voices inside of my head and the voice that tells me to be afraid is a different one from the voice that told me to get up; I am learning to distinguish between God's voice and the other voice.

One day in November 2004 whilst on the run, I received the news that my mum was ill. It was a Tuesday. My sister had called me telling me that mum was not responding to anyone. I cried and cried but decided to overcome any fear and go down to see her. When I got to her I asked her if she was alright. She told me that she was but I knew that she wasn't telling the truth. Her eyes were dim and she looked as though she didn't really see me even though she was looking at me. She was unable to walk and had become incontinent. That night I slept with her.

The next day my sister told me that we should take her back to the doctors as her condition was deteriorating and her right side had become completely numb. In Jamaica the medical services are not free so I had to borrow some money so that I could take her, but before taking her I said a prayer and asked God not to let her die yet. I then took her to the surgery but the doctor was away. I prayed again and asked God for direction. The taxi driver who had taken us to the doctor's suggested that I took her to the hospital. I followed his advice and when we got there she was seen by four different doctors. She was then admitted to a ward and I was told that she would require a brain scan and other tests. This would mean even more money which needed to be paid in advance of the tests, money which I did not have. The following day which was Thursday, as I sat by the side of her hospital bed, she had a heart attack. I couldn't believe what was happening. She had a second heart attack on the Friday whilst we were all by her side but I didn't give up. I believed my prayer and I believed that God had heard and he would answer me.

By now it was Saturday. I hadn't eaten anything yet I felt so strong. I knew that it was God keeping me and the hope of good news. I was unable to go to the hospital that day as I didn't have a single item of clothing to wear. That might sound strange but I had only travelled with the clothes on my back and I had washed them so they were drying. That day, I discovered that I had two missed calls on my cell phone.

Then my ex boyfriend came round and told me that my mum had been discharged. I hurried down to the hospital to find my mum sitting up. I combed her hair, got her ready and took her out of the hospital in a wheelchair. When we got home I asked one of the local pastors to come round and pray for her. His prayer worked and she was healed. The next thing I knew, she was up walking and talking. When the pastor prayed for her he got her to repeat the sinner's prayers. He asked her if she would accept Jesus Christ as her saviour and she responded that she would. She received her healing and today she looks as though nothing has ever happened to her.

My mum's healing has been my proof that God is real. How could I not believe in God? I wasn't a Christian but yet when I prayed to him, he did what I asked. He did it for me even though he didn't have to. What of the present? Well I've said the sinner's prayer myself and have given my heart to the Lord. God is keeping me and I believe in God and know that the future is in his hands. I need a job and a place to settle as I am still on the run. I want time for myself and I want to be able to sit down in a comfortable setting to read my bible. It will come. I have changed and God is working through me. At times I feel very lonely and alone in this life but I know that I am not really alone as my God has promised to never leave me nor forsake me and I know that he is forever by my side.

Chapter 5

Lesbianism

I felt the confidence of a man when I wore men's clothes.

Now the works of the flesh are evident which are:
Adultery, fornication, uncleanness, lewdness, idolatry,
Sorcery, hatred, contentions, jealousies, outbursts of wrath,
Selfish ambitions, dissensions, heresies, envy, murders,
Drunkenness, revelries, and the like;
Of which I tell you beforehand, just as I also told you in time past,
That those who practice such things will not inherit the kingdom of
God.

Galatians 5:19-21

Donnie McClurkin in his book 'Eternal Victim Eternal Victor' shared the well known testimony of his deliverance from the spirit of homosexuality. My story is of similar deliverance but from the spirit behind bisexuality and lesbianism. When I was around the age of eight I was introduced to my first lesbian romp when my foster sister and I took turns lying on top of each other rubbing against each other. This is probably where the seed of lesbianism was first planted and where the spirit behind lesbianism came into my life. It was a time when I was very vulnerable and impressionable. At around the age of fifteen, I started to drink alcohol and was exposed to 'blue' adult movies featuring lesbian episodes. Although I didn't engage in lesbian acts at that time, looking back I can now see that those movies had watered the seed that had been planted years earlier.

Years later, a boyfriend introduced me to group sex with his male cousin. I brought along a female and although there was no female to female involvement, I was aware of thoughts in my mind for such involvement at the time and having feelings of regret that this did not happen. During that period, I could also remember being carried back in thought to the episode when I was eight years of age. I shared with a subsequent boyfriend the thoughts in my head for a threesome involving a female and shortly thereafter a threesome was arranged. I also had subsequent one on one encounters with the same female. I had no conscience at the time that what I had done was wrong.

On becoming a Christian my whole attitude to such things changed and the Lord gave me the understanding that it was wrong and that I had been manipulated into those practices. Satan had influenced my thoughts and feelings and taken advantage of my spiritual ignorance. I never understood that Satan could steer us by our thoughts and feelings by making us become aroused by things we would not have been aroused by apart from his involvement. I even allowed Satan to exert influence over my preference for male clothing. I now know that he did this to support and reinforce the butch lesbian image and designs he had for my life. I felt the confidence of a man when I wore men's clothes and my approach to life was different.

However, Deuteronomy 22:5 says that, 'A woman shall not wear anything that pertains to a man, nor shall a man put on a woman's garment, for all who do so are an abomination to the Lord your God.' The scripture warns us that Satan will try to influence us in this area when it says that neither sex should wear anything that pertains to (i.e. marks off) the opposite sex, like clothing, shoes or a certain dress style, etc. I understand that this scripture does not address the simple wearing of clothes but rather the secret or expressed desire to be, or be associated with, or to act like the opposite sex. Now I am a changed person and my confidence no longer comes from wearing men's clothing but instead it comes from the fact that I am a child of God. Now my sexual direction does not simply follow the feelings of arousal but the word of God. I know that I may have battles ahead with a variety of issues but my mind is fixed concerning God's design for me as a woman.

The day after I had brought the issue of lesbianism before God and rejected the spirit behind it and asked God to deliver me totally, I was hit with a severe and disabling toothache. I had to contact the emergency dentist and when I was examined the following day he discovered there was no reasonable cause for the pain I had experienced. The nerve in the tooth was not the cause of the pain and the dentist could not fathom where the pain could have come from. I believe that it was an attack from Satan. If you too are planning to break free of similar lesbian urges then don't be surprised if something similar happens to you when you honestly take your issues before the Lord for deliverance. Even if a similar attack comes your way, you may nonetheless be assured that God will deliver you from the power of the spirit behind lesbianism if you truly wish to be free.

Chapter 6

Anger

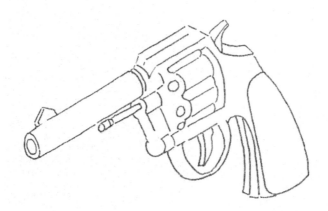

I was totally blinded by this anger, so much so that it caused me to behave in a manner which was totally out of character.

Then He said, 'I will Make all My goodness pass before you,
And I will proclaim the name of the Lord before you.
I will be gracious to whom I will be gracious,
And I will have compassion on whom I will have compassion.'

Exodus 33:19

No weapon formed against you shall prosper,
And every tongue which rises against you in judgment
You shall condemn.

Isaiah 54:17

Yea, though I walk through the valley of the shadow of death,
I will fear no evil; for You are with me;
Your rod and Your staff, they comfort me.'

Psalm 23:4

It was a typically hot, scorching Jamaican day but as I was returning from work I was walking into something that would change my life forever. My mother's partner had caused some damage to our family home so we had held on to his television as surety, until he had fully paid for the repair of the damage. This was the agreement or so I thought, but that day when I returned from work, I discovered that he had brought his police friends around to our house to settle the matter.

We were a quiet family and had no previous record of skirmishes with the police. In my eyes, this was a very serious matter and one that I felt I had to deal with. I was angry at what he had done and I must admit that there was more to my anger as I was a young man living a life of turmoil. My son's mother had told me that she would never let me see him again, and now this had happened. I exploded my anger on my mother's partner. He had never done anything to harm me, and he had not provoked me in any way, but so much anger had been building up inside of me. What he had done to cause the police to come to my mother's house was the last straw. This was 'THE' excuse for me to let out my anger and frustration at life on him. I was totally blinded by this anger, so much so that it caused me to behave in a manner which was totally out of character.

I watched as the police were coming out of the house and even though they had not quite yet left, I attacked him. I'm a slim person and this guy was almost twice my size. Normally I would not have attempted this but it was an erratic move based on impulse. Punches were exchanged, a fight developed and we wrestled on the floor. I rained blows to his face and I would have killed him if I could, after all I had almost given up on life and I didn't care what the outcome would be.

In the midst of all that was going on, I could hear movement behind me. What I experienced became the thing that was to change me forever. Suddenly I came face to face with police officers bearing guns and revolvers. They were pointing their weapons directly into my face. Looking at a loaded muzzle is like looking at death itself. And then it happened - click, click, click, click, click, click. I saw my life slipping away from me. For a few seconds I thought I had gone to hell and back. It was as though my spirit had left my body and I thought I was dead. I wasn't even able to cry out with what would have been my last breath, 'Lord have mercy!' I couldn't utter a word, but come to think of it I was not thinking about God so I didn't think about calling upon his name. I was ready and willing to face death with open arms at that moment, but something was wrong, I was still alive. No bullets had been released from the officer's guns. This was not a coincidence. How could six guns have jammed or have developed problems all at once? The impossible had happened. The only answer that I can give was that God was working that night and he had performed a miracle. I thought that the explosions from the guns would be the last sounds that I would ever hear on this earth. It truly was a miracle. I was alive and not dead! Yet even so, I was a bit disappointed at the knowledge of this fact. I thought that I was ready and prepared to face death at that very moment. As I look back now at my life, I can say that I'm glad of God's mighty intervention.

At this time, I was conscious of my mother, my sister and five other neighbours screaming 'Police!' and 'Murder!' Then as quickly as they had come, the officers re-holstered their pistols and walked away without even arresting me for assault. That was something that I was clearly guilty of. There are both good and bad in the Jamaican police force but as a Jamaican citizen, if you value your life you don't mess with them. But that day I had made it quite clear that I did not care. I was able to get up and brush myself off. It didn't feel real, I was able to get up and walk with the living and not with the dead. After that event, I pictured people coming to my funeral. How would it have been for my mother to have watched me being shot dead? I'm sure it would have killed her. So many things were going through my mind, I did not get a chance to react; I couldn't. I felt as though everything was over in that very moment.

One of my neighbours told me afterwards that they didn't know that I was like that. But I wasn't really aggressive. I was just young and angry with life. How could the police have done this to me? I was furious and the same night I went to the police station to make an official complaint about the behaviour of the officers. The officer on the desk told me that my mother's partner had already been into the station and had made a long statement about me. From what he had told the officer, he had given the impression that I was a dangerous man and I was told that it was lucky that I was not behind bars. One of the officers then spoke to me and told me to go home.

The next day I heard the report that my mother had been physically assaulted by her partner. I blamed myself for what had happened to her, you see maybe if I had not attacked him, then he would not have hit my mother. The anger that was within me had been fuelled and my mind began to consider revenge. He had done this to my mother, now he had to pay for his actions. A close family member told me that I needed to fix up myself. I knew that this meant going to visit someone in the community known as the 'Obeah Man', the Wizard or the Necromancer. He would have performed the ritual of giving me a bath or some other evil deed. I don't know why but I flatly refused, I knew that if I had taken this route, I would have sold my soul for eternity. I didn't have a relationship with God but somehow I knew that this was not the way to go. If I had taken this advice, I would have been blighted for life looking down the road of destruction.

Instead I got a machete which I planned would be my weapon of attack and as I was about to go to the guy's house, I was stopped by a neighbouring policeman who was able to reason with me and take it from me. I was preparing for a confrontation with the enemy, I didn't even care if I won or lost. I then armed myself with a knife and a pick ice but it was as though he was doing everything to avoid me. He wouldn't come out of the house. I thought that because he was a big guy, that his ego and pride at being beaten by a smaller man would cause him to want to get back at me, but nothing happened. Many of those who were close to me were not aware of the impact on me from what had happened. I began to secretly plan to harm him, seeing that he was not willing to face me man to man. I spent night and day thinking of how I could take my revenge. I went to see a friend who was a political activist and asked him to get me a gun. It was within his power to do so, but he refused. How could he as a friend refuse me a weapon? He could not be a real friend. My thought pattern had become warped. Another friend offered me an alternative solution. I could get friendly with him and make him my drinking partner, and then when he had become relaxed with me, I could poison him. This idea was not appealing to me although my mind ran through a million other ways that I could get back at him.

I decided that the best way to get back at him was to buy some petrol, make some cocktail bombs and throw them into his house whilst he was sleeping. He would burn to death. This was it, this would work, the perfect plan; I had made up my mind and I was ready. With the plan in mind, one night I was in my house having just finished watching the Sunday night movie, I got up to go into my bedroom. I drew the curtain to enter the room and immediately felt the overpowering presence of God. I say overpowering because I remember going down on my knees and it was as though I was floating. I can't even remember my knees actually touching the cold floor. It was an amazing experience. Everything that was in me just came out and I began to tell God how I was feeling. I opened up about the emptiness, the hopelessness and loneliness of my life. There was a void, a vacuum in my life and somehow I knew that it needed to be filled and only God could do this. At this very moment something happened to me and I immediately abandoned my mission of revenge. It had reached a point where God said, 'Enough is enough.' I was not thinking about

God yet he had chosen to visit me in my very moment of need. I knew that I did not deserve God's love and that I wasn't worthy of it, yet he chose to spare my life from the clutches of certain death, and even to visit me personally. I have never had an experience like that since and maybe never will. With all that I had done, I was not expecting God's mercy or his intervention. I had truly been through the valley of the shadow of death but had come out alive.

I challenged God. If it was him who was speaking to my heart then he should show me a sign the following day. He did! The next day as I was travelling through town there was an open air evangelistic service taking place. I listened and remember the preacher asking if anyone would like to give their heart to Jesus. That was the sign. I immediately walked forward and fully surrendered my life to Jesus Christ. Jesus came into my heart and changed me. At that very moment Jesus took away something which I considered to be an addiction, from me. I refer to it as an addiction as I seemed to have no power over it. I had for some time had a problem with stealing small things. I would often take things without even realising it. Usually I would not even want to take something, but it was just something that I did. I felt ashamed of my addiction as it felt as though I had no power to resist it, but when I got a touch from God it immediately disappeared. I said 'Yes' to Jesus and it immediately stopped. Stealing for me was a big struggle. If the Lord had not saved me, I could have gotten into big trouble. In fact when I said 'Yes' to Jesus other things happened too. The problems in my relationship with my son's mother changed and even the malice that I had been carrying for my sister for many years just dissipated.

It was not long afterwards that my mother gave her life to Christ, followed by my sister. In fact I can report that to date, all of the seven witnesses who were present at the time of the incident with the police have given their lives to Christ, so great the impact that day. They were witnesses to God's divine intervention and they were touched and had an encounter with Jesus Christ.

I take God's word and his scripture verses very seriously now. His word is real to me. God has been good. I know what a miracle is and I have seen God's intervention in my life. I've felt his goodness. Sometimes when I am on my own, I question God and ask, 'Why me?' But even though I question him, I am grateful and I am thankful to him. What is so special about me that he reached out for me? I was ready to embrace death with open arms, I thought it was all over for me and really I didn't expect to see the light of day. Sometimes it seems like it was all a dream but all I know is that God is good and that if he had not saved me that day, I wouldn't have life. There is nothing that I can do to repay God for his love towards a sinner like me, but the one thing that I am committed to do is to glorify him and tell of his goodness.

Chapter 7

The Lost Child

I agreed that this would be the best thing for her so I allowed her to go and I gave up my daughter.

> *If you endure chastening, God deals with you as with sons;*
> *For what son is there whom a father does not chasten?*
> *But if you are without chastening,*
> *Of which all have become partakers,*
> *Then you are illegitimate and not sons.*
> *Furthermore, we have had human fathers who corrected us,*
> *And we paid them respect.*
> *Shall we not much more readily be in subjection to the Father of*
> *spirits and live?*

*For they indeed for a few days chastened us as seemed best to them,
But He for our profit, that we may be partakers of His holiness.
Now chastening seems to be joyful for the present, but painful;
Nevertheless, afterward it yields the peaceable fruit of righteousness
To those who have been trained by it.*

Hebrews 12:7-11

At the age of sixteen, I was working as a waitress in a restaurant and bar in the Caribbean Island of Trinidad. That was my life, it wasn't the easiest but it was what had been ordained for me. One day whilst at the home of my sister in law, I met a guy who wanted to know if I had a boyfriend. I was excited, I didn't have anyone in my life at the time and I was flattered that a guy like this who was from Canada would be interested in someone like me. It felt good and when he invited me out, I did not hesitate to take up his offer. We began to spend time together and by the time I was seventeen years of age I was pregnant with his child. At first I wasn't aware that I was pregnant. I'd actually run away with him and moved in with him and his mother, and it was there that I remained until my first child was born. At the age of eighteen, I gave birth to a son. It was a difficult and complicated pregnancy as my son was overdue and was born with the umbilical cord around his neck. In fact the first two weeks of his life were spent in hospital.

My boyfriend was a womaniser and had gotten another woman pregnant so my dad disliked him. I'd always had a good relationship with my father and at times to me it felt like I was his favourite child. It was important to me to maintain our relationship so after having my son, I went to my dad and asked him forgiveness. I regretted what had happened and he was gracious and forgave me. However, I felt that my life was good and despite rebuilding the relationship with my dad, I went to live with my mum, and then eventually set up home with my partner. It wasn't long before I became pregnant again, and a year after the birth of my first son, I gave birth to a second son. I was nineteen.

Things began to change between my boyfriend and myself. He had started to do drugs and taking cocaine. I followed him and began to smoke cocaine and on one occasion together we binged for five days straight. I wanted our relationship to work because it had always been my dream to live a stable family life. I think that this was the key to all of my problems and my desires. My parents had been separated for some years and the man that my mum lived with was an abuser of young girls. I suffered sexual abuse from him so my dream had always been to live a life where I could live happily with my partner and my children in a safe environment, something that I feel that I didn't have as a child.

When I was eight months pregnant with my third child, I left my partner because of his womanising ways; it was not that I did not love him but I could not live in a relationship like that. I gave birth to a daughter and worked hard to maintain all three children. Life was difficult. I wanted a safe place for my daughter and I didn't want what had happened to me to happen to her. Then an opportunity was presented which would allow her to permanently leave me and go away to a foreign country where she could have a better life. When I asked her what she thought of the option she told me that it was what she wanted. I agreed that this would be the best thing for her so I allowed her to go and I gave up my daughter. That was the hardest thing that I've ever had to do in all of my lifetime, it was heartbreaking.

When my daughter eventually got her visa and left the country it hurt so badly, I had lost my child and my life was turned upside down. I did not want to be separated from her but I knew that it was the best thing for her at the time. My heart was in turmoil and I began to hide it the best way that I could through alcohol and smoking. I began hanging out and going out but not just for an evening, sometimes I'd be gone for a week at a time. I didn't want to go home.

At this time I was a Hindu but had started going to church. It was also at this time that I met a guy called Barry. He had a crush on me but at first I was not interested in him. He smoked weed and would talk about his life. He also had a girlfriend but he liked me and kept asking me out and one day when he asked, I finally gave in. I think that I must have been drunk or high at the time as I went with him to a hotel that night and I ended up having sex with him. Barry was my sister's employer and I felt so ashamed after first going with him. That night when he dropped me off at home, he told me that he really loved me and cared for me. I liked him but at the time I did not love him and I was afraid to get too deeply involved in another relationship. The only thing that I felt was anger at myself for what I had done. Even so I began to date him but he began to cheat on me and driven by the hurt, I decided to get my own revenge by cheating on him. I continued to drink more to cover the pain. I also found that I was blaming my children's father for the wrongs in my life. I felt guilty but I was so hurt and raged. One of my friends with cocaine ended up contracting AIDS, that's not how I wanted to end up.

Even so I know that God was with me throughout that time. Barry and I eventually split up but then ended up back together. However, I continued to cheat with another guy. My life was crazy and frustrating and for a period of about three years I was living with two men at the same time. I took out my rage on the guy that I was cheating with. He was nice and loving but the love he showed me was the love and longing that I had for Barry. I was blind to love.

It was my dream to settle down and have another daughter. I did continue to get pregnant but because of circumstances I miscarried and aborted many times. There was a dreadful period in my life when I was pregnant but the baby died inside my womb. I could smell the baby. I had been hospitalised and was grieving for the loss but I was sent home with the baby still inside of me. I returned to the hospital where this time they kept me in. It was awful. The baby was not coming out. I screamed and begged God to make the doctors come and take it out and eventually they came. This was such a traumatic time in my life. I cried to the Lord, I was lost, but yet I still ended up back with Barry because deep down, despite all that he was doing to me, I loved him. It seemed to be a love - hate relationship because I wanted to spite him and run away. Maybe if I did this, he would miss me and love me more.

It wasn't long before I was given the chance to leave him for a time when some people told me I could travel to England so long as I carried a parcel for them. This was the opportunity that I'd dreamt of and I didn't hesitate to take the parcel once the ticket had been purchased for me. But then out of the blue I received some bad news. My sister told me that Barry had died. I was devastated and my heart was broken at the death of the man that I loved. The logical thing for me to do would have been to cancel the trip to England but the ticket had already been purchased and it seemed that I had no choice but to travel. If I made the decision not to travel and carry the package I would have been left with a huge debt which I would have been unable to pay.

At this present time, even though I am hurting, good came out of my life. I was caught with the package of drugs and imprisoned in England. It was here that I realised that I'd had enough of my previous life and that things had to change. I gave my heart to the Lord Jesus Christ and was water baptised in prison. I have prayed that God will heal me emotionally and now I am praying and believing that God will heal me physically, you see I have been diagnosed as HIV positive. I believe that God can do it. I am also praying for my father, who is a Hindu that my life will be a testimony to him of the goodness of the one true and living God.

Chapter 8

Family

At the time that I became a Christian, six of my cousins and two of my brothers were in prison, two were jailed for murder and one is still serving a life sentence.

God is not a man, that He should lie,
Nor a son of man, that He should repent.
Has He said, and will He not do?
Or has He spoken, and will He not make it good?
Behold, I have received a command to bless;
He has blessed, and I cannot reverse it.

Numbers 23:19-20

At the age of sixteen I gave my heart to the Lord, it was 1995. I was baptised two years later. I was the only one in my mother's family that was a Christian. My family is large; my grandmother gave birth to seven children who have to date given her a total of seventy four grandchildren, great grandchildren and great great grandchildren. At the time that I became a Christian, six of my cousins and two of my brothers were in prison, two were jailed for murder and one is still serving a life sentence.

I was in a poor state when I became a Christian. I was addicted to drugs and alcohol and I was bulimic. I was also a self harmer who had attempted suicide twice and to cap it all, I had twice faced the ordeal of rape. This all left me very insecure and depressed. I was in and out of hospital all the time. My stomach was so badly damaged that it had shifted out of place and ulcers had formed all the way down my oesophagus. My intestines were also damaged. I went from bulimia to anorexia and was put under the care of psychologists at a local hospital. By the age of seventeen I was in a bit of a state.

During my years of being an addict I was very desperate and I used to steal from my mum and anyone else around so that I could get the money to buy what I needed. I would go through bins and ashtrays hoping to find something to smoke. I would take to school in a medicine bottle anything I could get my hands on including straight vodka, whisky, rum and brandy. I knew I could not make it through the day without a drink. I was so high, drunk and ill throughout my school years that I was referred to specialists for help. On completion of school I sat my exams and my grades were surprisingly good and I left school with nine GCSE's, miraculous I say. They were not marvellous grades but I passed them all the same.

I went to Sixth Form College as a Christian and God began to use me in a mighty way. I would get to college early in the morning and go to the chapel and pray each day during my break time. God began to clean me up and I began to fast regularly not touching any meat. God also began to develop my gifts of evangelism, prophecy and discernment. Many of my peers were becoming Christians through the things that God was doing through me. I set up the college's first choir and we ministered at events in the community and other venues. People were touched and converted through the ministry. Some of them are still Christians today. I left the Sixth Form College with three A- levels and went on to do a Joint Honours Degree in Criminology and Sociology. I passed them all without having to do any re-sits.

I look at my life now and say 'Praise God.' My family were not Christians but they saw the change in me. I never lied or hid any of my struggles as a Christian. I was honest and open with them, and through that they were able to see how God delivered me at every difficult junction. I had been brought up by my mum and when I came to church I found it difficult as no one on my mum's side of the family were Christians. They were still smoking, drinking, going out to parties and doing their own thing. Though I was close to my dad and my siblings, I had a distant relationship with the rest of his family. For years I prayed that God would save my family. I would come home and smell weed in my house and see everyone drinking and I was being tempted all the time. For a time I stopped going to family functions and consumed myself with church activities, but my family began to hate it. They felt as though I thought that I had become too good for them, shutting them out and never having time for them. I was running to every ministry and doing everything but I never made time for the ones who loved me and cared for me regardless. God told me to fix up! I changed and as soon as I started to spend time with my family and love them instead of preaching to them all the time, they began to soften. Now my entire household are Christians.

2005 was a precious year in which four of my cousins, two of my sisters, my grandma, my grandad and my brother all gave their hearts to the Lord and became Christians. My mother had given her life to Christ five years prior. Five of my family members were also baptised during 2005 and are now strong in the Lord. It was both a great and a difficult year for me as I had been engaged to be married, but due to circumstances had cancelled the wedding. I'd also suffered from a number of physical illnesses and lost one of my brothers. But I still have to say that God is GOOD! For the first time ever during Christmas 2005, most of my family who lived locally came together, both Christians and non Christians, and we prayed together, not to bless the food but we prayed over each and every one of our lives. On New Years Eve many of them were in church. For me that was precious because I know where we are all coming from and to see so many of them in church was a miracle.

Throughout 2006, the Lord has continued the work upon my family and has done even more than I thought he would and yes, I am excited. My brother who gave his heart to Jesus is being cleaned up and God is moving in him in a powerful way. He is to be baptised and he has been fasting, praying and encouraging me in the word of God. How awesome? At the start of the year his nephew, a young man who is also coming from the streets, gave his heart to the Lord. My aunt decided to christen her grandchildren and at the service two family friends asked to be prayed for. They then gave their hearts to the Lord. Three of my cousins also gave their hearts to Christ and my uncle who was a Rastafarian for over thirty years has begun to go to church with my family and God is working in him too.

To see what God is doing around me at the moment is overwhelming, I came to church alone but God has remained faithful to his word. There have been so many times when I looked at my life and asked God, 'Where are you, why is this happening and why do you allow me to go through so much pain?' The fire was hot and still is at times. I've felt isolated, alone, misunderstood, angry, bitter and many other things, but God has taught me that his ways are higher than mine. I have really had to anchor my soul in Jesus and lean not to my own understanding. God looks on the heart of man. Even at times, when I could hide what was going on inside me and fool those around me, God said, 'No, purify your heart, fear me, love me, want me, seek me with all your heart and soul, crave me, let me be the most important thing in your life and seek to impress me.' Now I know that as long as he loves me I will be just fine.

We must all be prepared to be purged and to say, 'Not my will but thy will be done', no matter how hard it's going to be. I surrender all. One thing I have learned is that if you are not a true Christian and not a true reflection of Christ, those you live with will be the first to know. We must always remember that Jesus feels everything we go through, he is there with us, and he never leaves us nor forsakes us. When I look at the lives God has touched, changed, healed and delivered through me, I am broken. I am so broken and grateful because he did not have to use me.

I am encouraged to love God and let Christ be seen in me by the way I love and treat people. It is important for people to be themselves and to be honest about who they are and where they are at. If we are the only light that our family and friends will see, we must make sure that it is burning brightly. We must keep praying and not give up as God is real, he is alive and he is still saving people. I have been called for a purpose, not just to have two point five children and get married and gain status, but to ensure that other people know who Christ is. It's an honour and a privilege to be called into his presence and acknowledged as his own. I thank you Jesus for loving me, wanting me, covering me and keeping me.

Chapter 9

Survival

We used to witness burglaries, drugs and a wide range of criminal activity but it was home, it was all part of life on the estate.

The Lord is my light and my salvation; whom shall I fear?
The Lord is the strength of my life; of whom shall I be afraid?
When the wicked came against me to eat up my flesh,
My enemies and foes, they stumbled and fell.
Though an army may encamp against me, my heart shall not fear;

Though war may rise against me, in this I will be confident.
One thing I have desired of the Lord, that will I seek;
That I may dwell in the house of the Lord all the days of my life,
To behold the beauty of the Lord, and to inquire in His temple.
For in the time of trouble He shall hide me in His pavilion;
In the secret place of His tabernacle He shall hide me;
He shall set me high upon a rock.

Psalm 27:1-5

I was born in Manchester of Nigerian parentage. Living with my mum, dad and older brother and sister, we prospered as a family so my parents made the decision to move back to Nigeria. But soon afterwards, things became very unstable so we had to make a hasty return to England. This time we moved to London, firstly to a family friend's home until we were granted our own home on an infamous housing estate. I was about five years of age. This is where it all began, 'survival of the fittest'.

The estate was renowned as one of the worst housing estates in the country and I lived there during the seventies and eighties and finally got out in the early nineties. However, although it was a notoriously tough estate, it was our home and the children who lived there were our friends. We used to witness burglaries, drugs and a wide range of criminal activity but it was home, it was all part of life on the estate. We lived there as a family. My brother was the eldest, then my sister and there was me. As siblings we were one year apart in age and then my younger sister was born when I was fifteen.

My older sister found life on the estate difficult to deal with. She was mild mannered and could not cope and eventually had a breakdown whilst she was at secondary school, and she lost her mind. Life bothered me but I was harder and headstrong and more able to cope. I even participated in some of the seedier things like shoplifting and going to raves and things like that. By this time, my mother and father had separated and my father went back to live in Nigeria. If the situation with my sister was not bad enough, the same thing happened to my mother. Two psychiatric cases in one family, it seemed that all of the women in my family were losing their minds. My sister eventually had to go into an institution and once even to prison because she stabbed someone, not because she was evil but because she was sick.

If I could say that I had a vice, it would be weed - ganja - marijuana. I smoked it from the time I got up in the morning until the time I went to bed. I was buying it in all forms; hash, skunk and black, I bought it in all measures. I just thank God that I never liked the smell of cocaine, to me it smelt like burnt tyres and it was a put off. I know that this is the only thing that stopped me from using it. Weed was my way of dealing with life and with everything that was going on around me and within my family. Praise God for as I share this story, I am coming up to my first anniversary of being drug free after over twenty years of smoking weed.

My mum had a lot of ups and downs in her illness. It was the best news ever when she told me that she was pregnant with my sister. I remember doing cartwheels because I was no longer going to be the youngest in the family. After the birth of my sister, my mum outwardly seemed to be stable but I realised that she was still struggling with depression. At one time she tried to take her life with sleeping tablets. I was nineteen and still living at home and it was me who had to call the ambulance. Social Services got involved and my sister was taken into foster care, she was four years of age. My eldest sister was in an institution, my brother had left home and I was left trying my best to look after my mum in such poor housing and social conditions. My mum would often start throwing things, shouting and even taking her clothes off and running about naked. It was hard as there seemed to be no resources available for people with mental illness, and in the area that I lived in there was a certain stigma attached to this sort of illness. For her there seemed to be no solution and maybe death would be the relief that she needed.

Suicide was something that I had witnessed. There was a family on the estate which lived in the flat directly below ours. Just before I was twenty one, I literally saw a friend of mine commit suicide. He could not face life anymore and he set his home and himself on fire. There was a big explosion. The irony of it was that his sister told me afterwards that he died with a smile on his face, even though his body had ninety seven percent burns. I didn't want to tell my mum the news as she had just come out of hospital, little did I know that she would later do it herself but by different means. It was December 1989 and I was twenty one and my little sister was six. My mother went missing for some time; she couldn't swim so she chose to drown herself in the nearby River Lea. The police came to tell me that they had found her body. I didn't know that she was going to do it and I still have her suicide note. 'Take care of your sisters as your brother takes care of you,' it read.

I wanted an angel to come and take care of things but that did not happen. I was still living all alone in the family home, the flat on the estate. I tried to get my younger sister back but Social Services said that she could not come back to live with me whilst I continued to live on the estate. At the time I was heavily reliant on drugs but I could still get to work, drive and do everything. When I think of it now, I cringe. I tried to get a move with the Local Authority but they wanted to give me another flat on the same estate. I became a bit more militant and got help from a solicitor to get my sister back. People would tell me to let an aunt or a relative look after her but I wanted my sister. I wanted to look after her and in 1992 I finally got a flat on a quite council estate away from the dreaded estate and I also got my sister back; I had peace of mind. I know what it is like to live on a run down, crime ridden council estate so I can never and will never ever turn my nose up at anyone.

Whilst living on the estate, the family of the young man who committed suicide would invite me to church. They were church goers but I would mimic and laugh at them for that. I had a really bad attitude. There was even a time when a lady would come and preach the gospel to me but I would be rude to her. How I wish I could see her again and apologise for my behaviour. By 1998 I had a partner. We had our problems but we made the decision to move back to my place of birth, Manchester to start a fresh life. My sister also moved with me. I wanted to have children but was taking fertility medication as I didn't think that I was able to get pregnant. You can imagine how overjoyed I was when the doctors told me that I was pregnant. I was told to go for an amniocentesis to test for Downs Syndrome but the results showed that all was well. At this time, I did believe in God and would thank God but I was not willing to give up any of my time for him.

At thirty six weeks of the pregnancy, I was admitted to hospital for high blood pressure. I had a lot of pressure at home, and my boyfriend and I were having a lot of arguments over his bad debts. The one good thing about being in hospital was that I couldn't smoke. I had still been smoking in plentiful amounts throughout my pregnancy, after twenty years of weed I couldn't come off it. One day during my time in hospital, my stomach began to feel strange. I thought it was a result of something that I had been given to drink. But then blood suddenly began to gush out of me. The nurses pushed me onto a bed and I could see them rushing around and there was a lot of frantic activity. I remember them listening to my baby's heart but they couldn't hear anything. I screamed at them. 'Save my baby!' That's the last thing that I remember as I was taken to theatre. I woke up to hear my partner say, 'Our daughter didn't make it.' That was October 27th 2000, the day my daughter Abicare did not survive.

This was to be the turning point in my life. Not my sister's illness, not my mother's suicide, but this. At first I was in shock. I was told that I was lucky to be alive. I had lost so much blood, if I had been at home when it happened I may not have survived. But that did not matter to me; all I wanted was my baby back. I just kept crying; I couldn't stop. I was able to hold her and I remember that she was still lukewarm. I needed comfort and people came along with comforting words. One of the midwives told me that she could not have children. The hospital cleaner told me that she also lost a child and in her day they just took the child away without her being able to see or touch it. These words helped me but they were not enough. I kept asking the nurses to bring her into the room even up to two weeks afterwards so that I could see her and touch her. She was cold.

Going home without my daughter was the hardest thing that I had to face. I lost so much weight that I looked as though I was anorexic. I did some crazy things, even going to the cemetery at three o'clock in the morning to see if I could raise her up from the dead, I was desperate. A friend of mine gave me a tape to comfort me by a preacher called T.D. Jakes. The moment I put it on, the question he asked seemed to jump back at me, 'Do you know that there is someone looking over your child?' He was talking to me and his words touched me. I began to watch the Christian channels on television. The programmes were my medicine. I could have lost my mind; I was nearly losing it.

I began to go to church to try to deal with the pain. I seemed to deal with family issues in London better than this situation in Manchester. I didn't want to exist but this was like my wake up call. I was back at home, still smoking and with no baby. What else could I do? I also had to deal with my partner who one day told me that I had killed his baby through my smoking. There was so much pressure and so many questions. The doctors did tests on me and they found out that I had a placental abruption so that the afterbirth had come away from my daughter. However, they told me that I might be able to have another child in the future, which at least was good news.

It was not long after that I discovered that I was pregnant again, so this time I stopped smoking as my boyfriend's comments continued to ring in my ears. My blood pressure was still high as I still had to deal with our relationship issues. In the twenty eighth week of the pregnancy I was at home in the bathroom brushing my teeth when I suddenly felt unwell. There were no doctors or nurses around and it was happening again, the only difference was me, in that I had begun to go to church and was watching the Christian television channels twenty four hours a day. I was again in a pool of blood. I began to pray, 'please Lord', 'your will Lord', 'help me Lord'. I was asking this of God and not of the doctors or nurses. As I lay in the ambulance, I continued to pray and pray and pray. I was scanned to see if the baby was alive. Yes, they found some movement but I was losing too much blood. Again I was rushed into theatre but this time I woke up to hear my boyfriend saying, 'We've got a son.' What beautiful words!

I called him Victor; Victor by name and Victor by nature. I couldn't see him that day but when I eventually was able to see him, I nearly passed out, he was so small. The woman whose baby was in the next incubator asked me what was wrong with me after all her child was just over one pound in weight at birth. On my release from hospital I visited Victor every day. On one visit I saw the family of the baby in the incubator next to Victor's rushing towards me. I knew it was bad news, she had lost her baby and I had to be there to help her get through.

God is good; he performed a miracle in my life. It was he who was in charge. It wasn't the doctors who saved my child, but God himself. That's the difference. I had called upon him and believed that he could do it. My faith was in him and not in man. What happened to my daughter had to happen, it was my turning point. I'll never turn my back on God. I've learnt too much and he's done so much for me. I must admit that shortly afterwards when I came home from the hospital after Victor's birth, I began to smoke again. But soon after I discovered that I was pregnant so again I stopped during this pregnancy. I realise now that God was weaning me off drugs gradually, but my final breakthrough came after watching a programme on television about a prison in the USA. I had become involved in ministry to female prisoners and had just returned home from a visit. I sat and watched a programme called, 'Engineering Super Max Prisons'. It was about a prison system within the prison system, a prison which was the worst of the worst, where prisoners were left to lose their minds. When I watched the programme, I had to thank God for the women in the prison that I had just visited. It made me realise that what I had to do was so easy and simple; all I had to do was stop smoking weed. From that day on I have not smoked and very shortly it will be my first anniversary. I am drug free.

I thank God that he has taught me about survival. True survival can only come through God. My life is now one of submission to him and in service to him. I continue to work with women prisoners and I was privileged recently to be water baptised inside a prison alongside prisoners. Praise God for survival, praise God for freedom.

Chapter 10

Rebellion

My attitude changed, it became bad and I became ignorant and arrogant. No one could tell me what to do. It was my time to rebel.

Enter by the narrow gate;
For wide is the gate
And broad is the way that leads to destruction,
And there are many who go in by it.
Because narrow is the gate
And difficult is the way which leads to life,
And there are few who find it.

Matthew 7:13-14

I'm twenty two years of age and I was brought up by my mum in a single parent household. In fact I am the only male sibling child and one of the few males in my generation of the family. Basically you could say that I am from a family of mainly females. Yes, I had male family members from my dad's side, but I rarely got to see them. There were two male family members from my mum's side but they were ten to twelve years older than me, but at least they were men that I could look up to. It was good having these guys around, these were the men of influence in my life and they were my role models. They were involved in gangs and street life so as a youngster they would give me sweets and the latest toys. Being around them was fun but they were not really positive role models. By the time I was twelve, they had been imprisoned and locked up; one sentenced to life imprisonment, the other sentenced to thirteen years. When this happened, I began to start moving around with male family members from my dad's side. My dad was an older man and my brothers were also much older than me. Their sons who were my nephews were nearer to me in age so it was to them that I began to get close. Sadly In 1996 one of my nephews to whom I looked up to was shot dead.

I was thirteen years of age in 1996 and it was a hard year for me. I desired the things that my mum was not able to afford. She found it difficult to make ends meet and my father was never around. With my family members now locked up in prison and my nephew now dead, my attitude changed, it became bad and I became ignorant and arrogant. No one could tell me what to do. It was my time to rebel. I began to smoke weed (cannabis). I started at first by stealing weed from my mum's boyfriend. My sister was going through a lot of her own stuff and she would get the blame for my stealing. I would take whatever I wanted but because I had stolen it, I never got to know the true value of it. I had no money and as my cousin's weren't around to give me money I began to go out and tax (rob) people and run off. At the end of that year, I began to sell weed and at the same time I was smoking a quarter of an ounce of weed a day. This was a lot of dope to smoke a day at this young age but I had gained a habit without the knowledge of the value of the amounts that I smoked.

I began to sell weed to my school friends and then began selling to the children of the neighbouring school up the road. I would make good money. Because I would go out of town to get my supplies, my weed became known as the best weed around, so I began to get a good reputation as a dealer and was selling to schools all around the area. Before going to school I would consume a quarter bottle of brandy and an eighth of an ounce of weed. I would be high, walking around like a zombie. I lived like this through most of my school years.

It was when I was fourteen that my brush with the law began and I had to appear in my first court case. I'd acquired a knife which I had taken from my sister's dad. One of my relatives had been riding up the road on his bike doing his paper round. He was looking at a guy who then challenged him and had asked him who he was staring at. My relative had a bad attitude and there was no way that he was going to back down with this guy who was much older than him. The guy therefore went to his car and got a baseball bat out of his boot. Wasting no time, my relative sped round to my house to ask me if I still had the knife. He arrived agitated and angry. I grabbed the knife and we started to walk round to the guy's house with the intention of stabbing him. As we walked through the local streets, crowds of our friends began to follow us knowing that something was about to happen. When we arrived at the house the man did not come out. Foolishly, we did not realise at the time that he had two houses on the street and we had gone to the wrong one. Before we had time to think, the man came out of nowhere and hit me on the head with a cosh. I fell down, my head was busted and all I could see was red. It hurt. A fight broke out and there was mayhem.

At the time of the incident, one of my cousins happened to be passing by in his car so when we told him what was happening, we got a surprised reaction. He told us to go home! I was angry at him because I thought that he would take some kind of physical action, but he didn't. When I arrived home my mum was frantic and she convinced me to go to hospital to get my head wound checked out. I didn't really want to go but I finally agreed, but little did I know that the people that we'd had the confrontation with were also there - with the police! I was identified and arrested for affray and violent disorder. Immediately after being attended to by the nurses, I was taken to the police station. By then it was 8pm in the evening and I was not released until 9am the following morning, thirteen hours later. My final charge was 'Actual Bodily Harm'. I got mad at the world. To me all that I had done was to come out of my house to help my relative, I hadn't done anything wrong but yet had got a busted head and then arrested.

My life in the fast lane continued and at the age of sixteen I went to visit to someone close to me who was in prison. I told him that I intended to start supplying weed to him in prison. He made it clear that I didn't have to but if I chose to supply him with drugs it would be because it was my own personal choice. I told him that it was something that I wanted to do. I remember the first time that I did it I was buzzing; I was happy that I could please him and do something for him. This became a regular occurrence. Besides taking the drugs into prison I was always getting into trouble at school. Whenever anything bad happened, it would seem that I would always be blamed because of my reputation as a disruptive troublemaker. One day at school, I got into an argument with a teacher. A window was later smashed and although it wasn't me who did the deed, I was blamed for it. The police were called and I was charged. More court cases began to follow as I continued to get into trouble but somehow I always seemed to get let off or cautioned. At seventeen, I began to cool off a bit as I didn't enjoy my run-ins with the law.

At the time, I began to chill with someone who belonged to a gang and through him I became more knowledgeable about life on the street. I also then began to chill with someone who was slightly younger than me. To help him with his business, I told him that I could hook him up with guns, weed and drugs, which I could get from my supplier. Unfortunately he radically got caught up with the gangs, chasing people and shooting after people. This was something that I wouldn't do. I would shift guns but not shoot them. I had a more laid back attitude to life and was into making money rather than into committing acts of violence.

I had done a lot in my life at such a young age but it was only at age of eighteen in 2002, that I began partying. In the past I'd not really had such a desire to go out. Despite all of the trouble and things that I had been involved in, I lived at home and my mum was strict. On my first occasion out, I didn't return home that night, I just stayed out and partied. It was that year that I went on holiday with my dad for the first time ever. Our destination was sunny California and I loved it. I met one of my two older brothers and other family members. I had always loved West Coast gangster rap, the likes of Snoop Dog, Ice Cube and Tupac, so this was a dream trip for me. My intention for the holiday was to just drink as much alcohol and to smoke as much weed as possible. It wasn't a problem getting supplies and I was supplied with 'hydro', 'hygrade' and 'chronic', which were all forms of cannabis. I got drunk on Alizé and I moved around with the thugs; this was truly the 'gangsta' life.

I was unaware that my brother had been watching the amount that I was drinking and smoking. He had become concerned and spoke to my dad about it. In the States, it is illegal for anyone to buy alcohol until the age of twenty one so I was breaking the law. They told me that I was drinking and smoking too heavily. I responded by telling them that I was bored. In England I would not have been breaking the law by drinking as the legal age limit is eighteen. This is what I did at home. The consequence was a big bust up with my dad. Here he was trying to tell me what to do and how to run my life yet back at home he had never been there for me. To make matters worse, he put the blame for the breakdown of our relationship onto me. In his eyes the failure of the relationship was due to me not visiting him and maintaining contact. To cap it all he took my weed from me and hid it. That did it for me, but it did not stop me. More trouble was to follow when I was caught with a 'spliff' at someone's house after being warned of carrying and using drugs. My dad and my brother were called and we had our second big bust up. I ended up staying for the remainder of the holiday at the home of another relative. She was good to me; I think that she understood me and whilst staying with her, I was able to enjoy the final part of my holiday.

Going to the USA changed my outlook on life. On my return to England I wanted bigger and better things. I was drinking and smoking more and I even began to take other drugs into prison, because I knew that I could make much more money than I would if I was selling it out on the streets. I was taking in heroin, cocaine and ecstasy. The people that I supplied were partying in prison on the drugs and I was partying on the outside with the money. When I was twenty, my main supplier of weed was sent to prison. He meant a lot to me and one day I decided to take some weed into the prison for him, but my luck ran out and I was caught red handed. There was no way out of this one so I owned up to the act. My solicitor advised me that I would be looking at receiving a custodial sentence and my trial date which was set at Friday 13th December 2005.

When the day of the court hearing arrived, I prepared myself for a custodial sentence with my clothes, my cigarettes, hifi and weed. When I walked into the court, there was a black judge and two white students. I call them my white angels. The judge was from Liverpool and he had come to the court to sit in for another judge who was ill. Against all of the odds I walked out without a custodial sentence. Instead he told me that he was going to give me a chance, so instead of going to prison I was sentenced to do community service. I was grateful and told him that I would start to behave myself and live right. The problem was that even though I meant it at that very moment, as soon as I got home I went straight back into the lifestyle that I had been accustomed to and settled back into the same old bad habits. Nothing had changed.

I began to travel to London with the person who I used to hook up with guns and the two of us also continued to take drugs into prison. We were paid well; one rich guy in prison would give us lumps sums of between £900 and £1500 a time. Together we amassed about

£20,000 in cash. We bought cars, had meals at luxury restaurants and began to live a lavish lifestyle. We quickly went through £10,000 through partying, and buying designer clothes, watches and living lavishly. By the end of that month we'd actually squandered £20,000 to £30,000. We spent money as though it was never going to end. But one day I got a call from hospital from my friend who said that he had just been shot. I was scared; these were bad boys who had shot him. I went to see him and saw where the bullet had penetrated him. He was lying there just staring; I told him that he could cry if he wanted to. He told me that he was in pain, that it was hurting and that it was burning. I was angry as this was someone who was close to me and meant a lot to me.

The result of all of this for me was that I decided to spend more time away from the crowd and more time out of town. Up until then, I had dealt in ecstasy but never had a desire to use it. One day someone asked me to get some for her. She'd at first asked me for 'Wiz' which is an amphetamine, but I'd told her that I was unable to get hold of any. Instead I gave her ecstasy and she told me to join her in taking some of the pills. I refused. However at the time my mobile phone was out of credit so we came to a silly agreement; she would pay to put credit on my phone if I took the ecstasy with her. After taking my first pills I remember driving and at first thinking that I couldn't feel anything. However, at the same time I kept telling those that I was with that I was getting hot. I remember listening to Mary J Blige's 'No More Tears'. I really felt the song and the ecstasy made me feel good. I partied all night and took a total of eight pills. I was also drinking champagne and alcohol, as well as smoking weed. I was buzzing and didn't go to sleep for two days, we just moved from club to club. I was later informed that I could have killed myself by taking such a large dosage of ecstasy.

I continued to get away from Manchester squandering the money that I earned so easily. One day someone asked me to look after some of his weed for him. I did not hesitate in agreeing to hold it, putting it in a sports shoe box in my bedroom. The problem was that the police had my details over another minor matter and decided to carry out a raid on my house. They found the weed which I'd actually forgotten that I was holding and they also found scales, snap bags that I used to sell drugs and also some cash. I was arrested and charged with intent to supply. My immediate response was to lie and tell the police that the scales and snap bags belonged to other people. I also told them that the weed was for personal use and was bought with money that I had made from selling clothes which was something that I had started to do.

When the case finally got to court my charges had been dropped to a lesser charge of 'Possession'. As I'd already pleaded guilty to this offence I was given another Community Service Order, this time for 80 hours. All I could say was, 'Thank you Lord'. I thanked God but I was ignorant as to which God I was thanking. Was he the God of Islam or the God of Christianity? This was a wake up call! In recent times I had crashed two cars that I part owned, as well as a number of rental cars. Also, someone close to me had been shot and I had been in a car which had been followed and shot at. Yet even though the driver had been a poor driver, he had managed not to crash the car and on inspection there was no damage. With this court case it was clear that things were beginning to go down hill for me. I was twenty one years of age. It was then that I started to take a back seat from the partying. In the past I had even had friends come over from Ireland to buy drugs and guns from me. I'd make good money from them as we could always charge them a bit more than the going rate, but all this was to now start to come to an end.

Throughout this period, my mum who had become a Christian told me that she was pleading the blood of Jesus over my life. Also my sister who was a born again Christian had been talking to me about God and telling me to look to God. I used to be argumentative with her and challenge her as to the identity of God. They would both pray for me continuously and in November 2005 I was introduced to a girl who had converted to Christianity from Islam. After speaking to her, my eyes were opened to Christianity. By then I had already decided that there was a God, but had been confused as to who God was. In speaking to this young woman, I realised the God of Christianity was real and alive and that it was him who had brought me through so far. I was feeling empty and down with the partying. I had a thirsting for something more which the partying and drugs could not fill. After speaking to this girl, I began to go to church and went to a see a Christian play and immediately afterwards I decided to commit my life to God.

I must admit that the partying did not stop straight away and I still had many of the same desires. But at the start of 2006, the local church began a twenty one day fast. I'd made the decision to do it along with my mum and my sister. The night before I had been out partying on ecstasy and had arrived home at about 6am in the morning. The prayer meeting started at 8am. I was hung over and dehydrated so the first thing I did when I got there was to ask for a drink. At first I was refused but then I was given a cup of mint tea. I had two sips then left the rest. By the end of the twenty one day fast I had stopped smoking weed. During that time I also went to a men's retreat and was touched by God. On becoming a Christian, I needed to know how I was now going to live and survive as I'd spent my whole life hustling. I told God that I would not hustle anymore so I needed an alternative. God proved himself to me and saw to it that I was okay in the short term and for some reason people who had owed me money which I had forgotten about began to pay back the debts.

I don't know what future plans will unfold for me but I know that God is going to bring me through. I'm going to college at the start of the next academic year which is something new to me. I know that it is God who is going to bring me through. As a new Christian I must admit that I have at times fallen back into my old ways and have smoked weed. However I realise that because I started smoking at the age of eleven, I have an addiction which can only be broken by God. It is something that I am constantly praying about. I also know that I will fall if I do not feed my spirit so I have learnt to do more than just go to church on a Sunday. At the moment I attend three bible studies a week and I have started to go to a prayer meeting with my mum. I am feeding my spirit. I have had bad weeks and on one occasion I got into an argument with a guy and slapped him. On that occasion I had to go away to London to clear my mind, but as soon as I got back I went straight into church activities.

I have since been baptised with the Holy Ghost and feel the power of God within me. I feel the happiness and have a peace of heart and mind that I never had before. I know that the key to my faith is to believe and have faith. As Christians we will always fall but it's important to come back fighting. I thank God for saving me and coming into my life. He has changed my destiny and I have a future.

Chapter 11

Rejection

I had spent my life feeling rejected by everyone, my mother and father, my grandmother, and those people who used me as cheap labour. I was bitter.

> *The Lord is my shepherd; I shall not want.*
> *He makes me to lie down in green pastures;*
> *He leads me beside the still waters.*
> *He restores my soul.*

Psalm 23:1-3

There is therefore now no condemnation
To those who are in Christ Jesus,
Who do not walk according to the flesh,
But according to the Spirit.

Romans 8:1

At the age of two, my mum gave me up to be cared for by my father's parents. My father lived in the States so was I taken from my home in Kingston, Jamaica to live with my grandmother in Central Village in the Parish of St. Catherine. I was to grow up in poverty in a home where there was very little. Furniture was scarce and we had no chairs and tables in the home which had a shared a yard with our neighbours. I had one brother who would beat me and ill-treat me constantly, yet for some reason he was favoured above me by my grandmother. But I did have one special person in my life, and that was my great aunt, my father's aunt, whom I called Aunt Granny.

I clearly remember a time in my life at the age of eight when my grandmother used to go to the local Spanish Town market to sell chocolate. She became ill so I became her hands and feet. She taught me how to mill the chocolate and get it ready to take to the market. I quickly grasped the business and eventually at the age of ten, I took it over and began to do the selling to make money, which I used to look after her and my Aunt Granny. I was a child. Up to that point my Aunt Granny had helped me to go to school. My clothes were ragged and I walked without shoes. I had no personal belongings of my own, even knickers, which people take for granted. I had none of these luxuries. I'd attended a basic primary and an all age school but now at the age of ten, I was to leave school never to return. There was no help for me and I had no one who was there for me.

As a child I was a helpful little girl, if anyone needed anything doing and asked me, I would always be available. This was a good character trait but I was often taken advantage of and used by so many people. I carried on the business until I was fifteen when it had begun to decline, as it was difficult to get chocolate to sell. Eventually the business collapsed and we became poorer and poorer. My Aunt Granny sold things in the yard and one of her customers allowed me to go to work in her food shop, washing the pots and dishes. She was a nice lady called Miss Dortmund. She saw that I was a good worker so she began to show me how to cook and she began to look after me. Her daughter would buy me clothes from the USA. Besides my Aunt Granny, nobody had ever looked after me or cared for me in this way before. I was trustworthy so I began to do the waitressing work in the shop and get a bit of money for myself. At that time, I also looked after my cousin's children in exchange for food, but eventually my cousin moved away and stopped bothering with me.

Miss Dortmund took me in as a family member and I stayed with her for a few years. I also began to sell cannabis to make additional money to help me to look after my Aunt Granny who had become very ill. I looked after her, bathing her, dressing her and cleaning her house. My Aunt Granny was the one person who showed me what love was. I had spent my life feeling rejected by everyone, my mother and father, my grandmother, and those people who used me as cheap labour.

I was bitter because of the way I had grown up living in poverty. I was selling drugs but through it all I held onto my integrity and dignity and did not let people especially men, take them away. On one occasion my friend's brother tried to rape me. God didn't allow him to have his way with me. We fought and fought and I managed to get away. Thank God it didn't happen. There were some times in my life that I felt helpless but I overcame.

As a child my grandmother and my Aunt Granny would take me to the local Catholic Church as well as to the 'Pukka' Spiritualist Church. On the day of a 'pukka' water baptism, the neighbourhood would be woken up by the pulsating sound of the beating of the drum. I would run outside and join in the procession to the river to witness the baptism. These were good memories. I enjoyed going to church, there was something in me that made me believe in God, although I did not understand anything about him because there had been no one to teach me. As a teenager, I would dream about Jesus but I had no understanding.

At the age of nineteen, whilst living back at my grandmother's home my father fell ill. I think that he had been shot and had problems with his feet so for that reason he came to live with us. This was the first time that I had seen his face and I remember thinking that he looked old. He had previously sent me some old clothes but I had rejected them, I didn't want them. He came with nothing and he wanted to take over the house but my brother would not let him, after all my brother had been the man of the house for all of these years. There was a lot of quarrelling over land but I wanted none of it. My father came to Jamaica with a pension but I never saw any of it. The only thing that I ever took from him was a towel but he behaved so badly that I gave it back. I would sometimes cook for him so he would at times acknowledge me as his daughter but eventually he got married to a young Jamaican girl and left us.

I still continued to help Miss Dortmund and got money from her. I also joined a gang of which I was the only woman and I would get involved in fighting and other activities. Something that really impacted me was when one of our gang members became a Christian. He came to us and told us that he'd had a dream about hell fire and told us that he was going to get baptised the following day. I knew that if he were to get baptised that we would lose him to the church and he would stop visiting us. I could see rejection staring me in the face again so to protect myself, I gave him the ultimatum that if he were to get baptised, then he could no longer come back to see us. I gave him a choice between the gang and God. He chose God, but the wonderful thing was that he would still come to visit, even though he stopped doing the things that we were doing.

As time went on I continued to move from place to place because of the fact that I could help people in their homes. I would visit a family member who was a hairdresser from the Molynes Road area in

Kingston. It was these experiences that really brought home to me the poverty that I lived in and the ghetto life that I had become used to. Seeing her home made me see how much better life could be. I had to be a survivor, ghetto life would not consume me, and I had to keep my self-esteem.

It was during this time that I fell pregnant and gave birth to my first child Samantha. Life with a child was difficult. I met Roy and became pregnant and at first when I told him of my pregnancy he rejected me along with his family. There was no one there for me to talk to or to share with, I had to go through it all on my own. I couldn't go back to live with my Aunt Granny as there was no room; she had one bed but she was ill and incontinent. Roy was a cabinetmaker and made beautiful pieces of furniture, which he would sell to the local stores. When I first met him I felt no love for him, I didn't know how to love and care for anyone besides my Aunt Granny. My heart had become like a rock stone. Samantha was ill at birth so I had to leave her in hospital for two weeks and Roy was nowhere to be seen. I decided to find out why he had not visited us. I was used to accepting rejection so I went to see him and said what I had to say and then left. One day when I was at my grandmothers, he called around and gave me $1600, which at that time was a lot of money. I was independent though so did not need to rely on him.

Miss Dortmund had taken me and the baby in; she took Sam as her God daughter. It was good to live in a nice house with a clean bed and I was able to start having my own possessions including shoes, knickers and other things that I had not had in the past. Roy visited a few times then one day he asked me to live with him in Maypen. I ran it past both Miss Dortmund and my Aunt Granny. They asked me if I was sure it was the right thing to do and I agreed that I would to move to live with him, but would come back if things didn't work out.

However before I was able to move my Aunt Granny fell ill on the day before Sam was due to be christened. It was Christmas Eve and I was nineteen. She was dying and I watched her on her deathbed as she fought to survive and live. She was breathing heavily and struggling and I remember asking her if she was going to leave me. She told me that she wasn't. I'd never seen anyone dying before but I knew that she wasn't going to stay with me, that she was going. I asked a neighbour if she was dying and she confirmed what I already knew. My Aunt Granny had cared for me and it was for this reason that I had supported her and cared for her. I had been determined to do for her that which she had done for me. My mother knew where I lived but never came to see me and I had sisters who had nothing to do with me, but yet there was still something within me that enabled me to care for my Aunt Granny. She took her last breath, the undertaker was called and I watched as they took her away in the white sheet. I cried.

I took Sam to the funeral. I loved my Aunt Granny; she had shown me so much love. I felt rejected, I knew that there was no one else for me and I was left on my own. Rejection is not easy to deal with especially as a girl child, having no one to look after you and teach you the essentials of life. I decided then that the best option was to go and live with Roy. For the first year or so he was good and behaved right, but I was disliked by his family. I think that the problem stemmed from his mum who thought that she was going to lose out because we were now his priority.

Roy set up a work shop in the yard of our home with his friend and his brother. After a while I began to see a change in him. He would go and visit the home of a girl who lived across the yard, and eventually I started to hear that he was having a relationship with her. When I questioned him about this behaviour he would begin to argue. I felt discouraged at the fact that he had stopped showing me any respect, so I made the decision to leave him and go back to Miss Dortmund. It was at this point that I found out that he had a temper and he began to beat me and became violent towards me. Not only would he beat me with his hands and fists, but he would use whatever instruments or tools that he could find. There were so many times I would wake up in severe pain and with my body swollen and bruised after his regular beatings.

By now I'd had my second daughter Charlene and we had moved to the Denbigh district of Maypen. I was still with Roy, maybe because what little self-esteem and self-respect I had, I had lost. He would do whatever he wanted to do to me including choking me to the point where I would end up having to fight for breath. After one such incident I had to go to the doctors to check my eyes which had been injured. He would get jealous if he ever saw me talking to another man. I wanted to leave but always ended up staying. The one person who cared for me was my Aunt Granny, but she had gone. I had a third daughter, Kim. As Roy went about with his brother to dancehalls, I would stay at home and look after the kids. I was stuck but couldn't say anything to him. I don't know what it was that was causing me to stay.

One day, out of the blue and despite his behaviour towards me, he asked me to marry him. As you can imagine, I turned down his proposal as I knew that he could eventually end up killing me. There was a church at the top of the road so I suggested to him that we should go and get counselling from the pastor. He agreed so although I went to see the pastor to make the appointment, when the time came Roy didn't attend. Because of my lack of schooling, I had little understanding of many things, but I began to get wisdom. I had an old battered bible so I would read Psalm 61 through my tears. I knew there was a God and I began to pour out my heart to him. I needed to know why everyone including this man, treated me the way they did. I needed answers. I couldn't take it any longer, living in a house with a man who had even stopped speaking to me.

One Wednesday evening I picked up the courage to tell Roy that I was going to leave him and go back to town. He told me that he was going to change but that night he beat me severely. I decided to stay at a girlfriend's house but he came round and as I stood there in pain and with swollen lips, he told me that never again would anyone ever hear that he had beaten me. I went back to our home the following night to talk to him, I was black and blue. I had this feeling that I should stay on the veranda and not enter the house, so I sat there in the chair whilst he stood by the door to the house. We talked and he said that he didn't know why he did the things that he did to me. All I wanted was to escape, I couldn't give him another chance as I knew that he would kill me. As he was speaking to me he kept going into the house. I didn't think anything particularly out of the ordinary as I thought that he was just going to the bathroom. Unbeknown to me, he had recently bought some kerosene oil and little did I know that each time he went into the house, he was drinking it.

I remember the last time that he went into the house and shut the door; I sat there waiting for him to return. Again I thought nothing of him disappearing until I heard a thud as though something had dropped inside of the house. I knew that the kids were sleeping so it couldn't be them. He had closed the front door so I was unable to get into the house that way, so I went to another door but that door was also locked. I began to shout his name, I wondered what was going on, I couldn't understand. Eventually he opened the door and walked past me. He had a belt around his neck but for some reason I couldn't bring myself to ask him if he was trying to kill himself. The words would not come out of my mouth. I went into the room and saw a belt hanging from the ceiling then I watched him as he entered the room. He told me that he was just looking for something; he had his penknife in his hand. I asked him what he was doing but something was telling me to get out. I ran out of the house and began screaming to a friend around the corner. 'Michelle, I think he's going to kill himself!' 'No!' she said. I ran back and as I put my foot on the first step, I saw him hanging. Our four year old daughter Sam was standing beneath him.

Roy had stood on a chest of drawers and then moved it. I shook him and grabbed his hands and screamed in terror for my neighbours who began to gather, I just wanted them to cut him down. I ran out in shock and my neighbour Michelle had to hold me as she thought that I would take my own life. I asked my daughter if he had said anything and she said that he had told her to look after her sister Charlene. When the autopsy was completed, it was then that I was told that he had been also drinking kerosene oil. I can't describe how I felt.

Despite all that he had done to me and even though I no longer loved him, I had the same feeling of rejection as I did when my Aunt Granny died. I hated Roy with a passion because of his treatment towards me and as I began to move on with my life, I carried the hate, I hated every man. Roy had done nothing for us but he had left me with a heavy burden. At times it was difficult for me, it was as though people including his family were pointing the finger at me like it was my fault that he was dead and that I was the guilty party. All that I had wanted to do was to leave him because of his treatment towards me; I had not wanted him dead, after all he was my children's father.

God had a plan for my life but I didn't know what it was and I was still searching for somebody and something. As time went on I began to rebuild my life and met another man, Amos who was caring and together we had a daughter, my third child. Because I had been struggling financially, Sam and Charlene had gone to live with their father's parents but Amos supported me where he could and helped me out with the children. Later I found out that Amos was not a single man as he had first claimed but even though I didn't like this, I accepted the situation as he treated me better than Roy had ever done. I could talk to him and he would respond in a positive way, giving me direction for my life. Through our relationship I began to have dreams of getting a house, or travelling abroad. I'd never had dreams before and I was learning much from him. I felt comfortable despite the fact that he had someone else.

It was whilst in the relationship with Amos that I was to have a life changing experience which would draw me to God. One of the local shopkeepers died. My friend and I were going to the wake and we were getting dressed and ready whilst waiting for a vehicle to take us. We could hear beeping outside but we were not quite ready at that moment. A car had arrived first and I remember my friend being irritated and commenting that if they beeped their horn one more time, we would not be going. Anyway, by the time we had come out of the house, the car had already gone so we got into the following truck. My friend said to me that she felt funny, that her heart had leapt but we dismissed it and put it down to the stuff that she must have been smoking. As we were driving towards our destination, we noticed that the road was jammed with traffic. This was unusual for this time of the day. There seemed to be so much movement and commotion so we asked the people around if they knew what was happening. We were told that there had been a horrific collision between a car and a train and that all of the occupants of the car including a baby were dead. It was only when we arrived at the wake that we discovered that the vehicle that had been involved in the collision was the car that we had planned to travel in. We rushed to the hospital to witness the full extent of the indescribable injuries that our friends had incurred. Only one person survived. She was the mother of the baby, and daughter of the man whose wake we were attending.

At the discovery of this dreadful news, my friend shouted out, 'God is good!' She saw that God had saved us and she praised and thanked God that we were alive. It was due to his divine protection that we had not gotten into the car and she saw that his hand was upon our lives. My friend immediately made the decision to surrender her heart to the Lord and was baptised the following Sunday.

On the day that we were due to go to the funeral my friend began to minister to me and talk to me about God. She told me that she thought that I should get baptised and that God had saved me for a purpose. I had planned to wear a white suit to the funeral and as I was ironing it, in my mind I began a conversation with myself. It was like I was talking to someone, yet there was no one else present but me. It troubled me. It was as though there was a voice telling me to pick up my bible and go to church. There was a battle going on in my mind. 'I'm not going', I said. 'I'll have to give up all that I have.' No one else was there but these thoughts were going round and round in my mind. I put on the suit then grabbed my bible and said, 'Okay, I'm going but if anyone looks at me I'm leaving.' I walked into the church and grabbed the backseat then I began to cry uncontrollably, I don't know where it all came from. There was an altar call and as the pastor was praying, I walked to the front and dropped onto my knees. I couldn't dry my tears, they just kept flowing. I remember the evangelist saying to me, 'Jesus is calling you.' I was touched by God and that evening I went back to the church and went through an hour of struggle looking at what I would be leaving behind. But good came through and eventually I surrendered and gave my heart to the Lord and made a decision to get baptised the same night.

Since that time much more has happened to me and I could write a book. God made a way for me to move to England. I've been imprisoned and released and I'm currently separated from my own children, but God is good and I have no regrets at my decision to follow the Lord. At times I still feel rejected, but I've been able to accept God's love for me. God has taught me to love, to have compassion and to be able to forgive those who may have wronged me. I've had a life full of rejection where I've had no one to give me direction but thank God for Jesus, he is my Shepherd and he has restored my soul. He restored my heart and now I am able to love.

Yes, sometimes I feel unloved and even if a person shows me love it can be hard to accept because of my past experiences. But rejection is in the flesh and not in the spirit and I'm a new creature. I've realised the importance of not letting the past affect my future. My life is in God's hands and he has taught me the one thing that I was unable to do and that is to love!

Chapter 12

Miscarriages

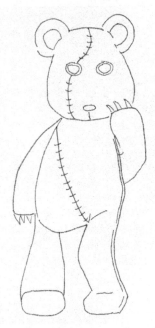

I was diagnosed as having extreme endometriosis. The usual treatment offered would be hormone treatment coupled with laser treatment, but because my tubes were so badly damaged I was told that this course of action would be ineffective.

> *Behold I am the Lord, the God of all flesh.*
> *Is there anything too hard for Me?*
>
> *Jeremiah 32:27*

> *No one shall suffer miscarriage or be barren in your land.*
>
> *Exodus 23:26*

I was married in August 2002 and it was my dream like other newly wed couples to have a child when the time was right. Our plan after marriage was to buy a house and then start a family. I had started a new job and wanted to wait a year until I had an entitlement to maternity leave before we started to try for a family, but my husband was determined that he wanted children as soon as possible. However, we jointly decided to start trying for a family after the first six months of marriage. It was only then that we realised that there might be a problem because when we began to try to conceive, nothing happened. After six months of trying, we decided to go to see our doctor. He told us that we should continue trying and if nothing happened in another six months, then we should come back to see him.

After three months nothing happened and this began to alarm us so we returned to see the doctor. Again he said that we shouldn't worry and that there was nothing wrong, it could even be that we were not conceiving because of the stress that we were putting ourselves through because we so desperately wanted a child. Nevertheless, our doctor sent us for tests and I had a laparoscopy where a camera was used to investigate my reproductive organs. When I woke up from the anaesthetic we were asked to go into a quiet room. My husband had been calm and we were not expecting anything to be wrong. The response that we got from the nurse when we asked her for our results shocked us. With her eyebrows raised she looked at the files and then told us that she could not give us any information. This was despite the fact that the results had been returned. Instead she said that she would need to get the consultant to speak to us.

When the consultant came into the room she sat down with a book and a pen and she showed us a diagram of the fallopian tubes. As a result of the investigations they had found that both of my fallopian tubes were badly damaged. During the exploration they had put a dye through the tubes to see how well it would travel but they had discovered that the tubes were bent in three places and the fluid had been unable to travel normally through them. On top of this they had discovered adhesions which were adding to the problem. In fact my tubes were even in danger of attaching themselves to other organs in my body. I was diagnosed as having extreme endometriosis. The usual treatment offered would be hormone treatment coupled with laser treatment, but because my tubes were so badly damaged I was told that this course of action would be ineffective and that there was nothing that could be offered to repair the damage. Instead I was offered in-vitro fertilisation (IVF) because there was a ninety five percent chance of me being unable to conceive naturally. But the downside with the IVF treatment was the cost. To carry it out privately would have cost around £3500 a time and there was no guarantee that I would get pregnant. We were told that maybe after two or three attempts I might get pregnant but this was not a definite. We estimated that we would have to spend at least £10,500. I was totally devastated! That day I went home and I cried and cried. I told my family; my mum was so supportive and my sister was my rock. My husband and I agreed there and then that we would do whatever it took to go through the IVF programme, even if we had to sell the house.

In the midst of the devastation and with the support of my husband, I took time out to pray to God. I had been attracted to my husband by a number of his qualities. Besides his handsome looks and his height, one thing that struck me about him was his unwavering faith in God. He said that we needed to pray and have faith and we needed to take time out to consult God on the situation, something that we had not really done effectively since the bad news. We therefore prayed and prayed and prayed.

The more I prayed the more I heard God speak. I became attentive, not just in reading the word of God but in listening to the voice of God. I did things that built up my faith including attending a conference where we were encouraged to find out what God was saying to us about our specific situations. We were then encouraged to believe it. God wants us to be fruitful and I now understood that this did not just relate to finances but to every aspect of life, including child bearing. I began to read scriptures where God had dealt with others in similar situations and I built up a faith so that I had an 'it is done' faith.

God continuously spoke in my spirit and also spoke to me through others including my pastor's wife. I decided to reject whatever was being thrown in my face and to believe only in the promises of God.

Every month I was expectant and anxious so you can imagine how happy and excited I was when I found out that I was pregnant. I told the news only to those closest to me, this was an important secret. Because of the problems with my fallopian tubes, there was a danger of an ectopic pregnancy. For this reason the doctors kept a close eye on me. Numerous tests were performed and one of the tests identified a problem with my hormone levels. Instead of increasing as they should in a pregnant woman, they were decreasing. For the safety of the baby I therefore had to attend hospital every forty eight hours to be checked out. On the Friday after I was first tested my own doctor advised me that if anything happened over the weekend I should go straight to the hospital. This advice was quite shocking to me, what did they mean, what could happen? I was so angry and upset and reacted in a likewise manner. As soon as I got home I told my husband what had been said. We did the thing that was most natural to us which was to get down and pray.

The very next day I started suffering from pains in my abdomen which felt like menstrual pains, and then I started to bleed. I went straight to the hospital where all I could do was to cry and bawl out. A blood test was taken which seemed to show that I was still pregnant. I just sat there hoping and praying that everything would be okay. On the Monday when the laboratories opened I was tested again. It was then that I was given the devastating news that my hormone levels had gone down and it looked likely that I had lost the baby. They also did a scan to confirm the devastating news. It was a time of total sadness for me.

My husband and I continued to pray, we had faith and thanks be to God I got pregnant again. Because of the problems with the previous pregnancy I again had to go to hospital every forty eight hours to have my hormone levels checked and it was again discovered that they were not going up sufficiently. This time I rested and took things easily. I'd gone longer into this pregnancy and at almost twelve weeks we went for a scan. All that myself and my husband needed was to see the heart beat of our baby to show us that it was okay. Praise God there was a heart beat which made us so positive and we continued to pray and believe.

Not long after on a Sunday morning when I came home from church, I felt similar pains as before, so I decided to immediately go to the hospital for a check up. This time we were not expecting any bad news. I was admitted and the following day one of the medical staff did a scan on me and I saw the baby. The radiologist's facial expression was extremely stern but this did not alarm me and I began to smile and rejoice with my husband who was holding my hand. Whilst we cheerfully watched he moved the equipment and told us to be quiet so he could concentrate. Just like that he said, 'Your baby's dead!' He was so harsh! We then had to wait for another doctor who confirmed this. They told me that there was nothing that they could do and that I would have to wait a couple of days for my body to realise that my baby had died. My body would then pass it out naturally. I was advised to return to the hospital when that happened.

My husband refused to accept this news and he went to the spare room to pray. He prayed and told the Lord that it was him who had shown us the baby's heartbeat so he demanded that the heartbeat be returned to our child. I cried and cried. The first day after my return home from the hospital I waited but nothing happened. On the second day again nothing happened and neither on the third or fourth day.

My mum was concerned that I might get septicaemia so on the Friday we went back to the hospital where it was decided that I would need to have an immediate emergency operation. I can't explain how I felt, it was horrible and I was scared. As I was being wheeled into the theatre it felt like I was being wheeled into a funeral parlour on my way to say goodbye to my baby. When I was given the anaesthetic it felt like I was standing over an open grave. It was so painful and my mind was going round and round wondering what they meant when they said that my baby would be discarded. Did it mean that they would flush it down the toilet? I was totally distraught!

I must admit that I did question God during this period of my life although I still had a deep faith in him and a belief that one day I would have a baby. I got tremendous support from others including my pastor and his family. His wife who I also call mum would cut out testimonies of people in impossible situations who had children and she even set out a diet plan to help me. She was indeed my rock. I was totally messed up by my first pregnancy and I was scared. With this pregnancy I was messed up because of the actual loss and grief and the fact that I would never hold that child or even know if it was a boy or a girl; I would not even be able to name it. I had no doubt that I would have children some time in the future and I was not worried about my condition but I was devastated by the loss. To this day all I have is the scan photograph of that baby.

God had told me that I would have children but he did not tell me about the obstacles that I would face before I got there. After the loss of my second child every month became a heart breaking time with so many false alarms and with me wishing and hoping that I was pregnant again. I was saddened by each negative test even though I knew that I would eventually get pregnant, and three years later it came to pass and I conceived. As you can imagine, I decided to keep quiet about this pregnancy. However this pregnancy was much different than the times before. I was very sick and sometimes would cough up blood. I spent around six months in hospital but I stood on the word of God. 'Behold I am the Lord, the God of all flesh. Is there anything too hard for Me?' from Jeremiah 32:27. Also 'No one shall suffer miscarriage or be barren in your land' from Exodus 23:26. These were the scriptures that I kept in my spirit. I also bought a number of books which strengthened my faith.

At each stage of the pregnancy I was told that the baby was okay but I became ill and developed a kidney problem. My kidneys were malfunctioning and the doctors advised that I should consider having an operation. However the safety of my baby was of paramount importance to me so I refused the operation. Instead, to help alleviate the pain, I was given daily Pethadone injections and because of the fact that I was not eating I would take four to five bottles of fluid a day via an intravenous drip. One Sunday when all of our visitors had gone, my husband and I both prayed together. He then left to go home and I was left all alone. Suddenly it was as though Jesus himself was present in my hospital room. As I looked outside of the window I could see the railings and in them I could see a perfect sign of the cross. I glanced back into the room towards the mirror and saw my toothbrush and something else which again presented the sign of the cross.

In fact I saw a third cross in the railings on my bed. It was as though Jesus was saying that he died for me so that I would not suffer and so that I would have life in abundance. I was in awe of his presence as it overtook me. I was due to take some painkillers as the Pethadone had worn off and it was as though the Holy Spirit was telling me not to take the medication. From that moment the pain disappeared. Tests had shown previously that my kidney's were severely dilated and that if I hadn't been pregnant, they would have operated upon me immediately, but I left the hospital three days later without having the operation and instead of getting worse, my kidneys improved.

I didn't return to the hospital again until my son was born. At the time of my admittance I was two centimetres dilated yet I was only in labour for two hours. The nursing staff thought that it would be a while before the baby came and it was suggested that I send my family away, but instead they stayed and an hour later I went into labour. My waters hadn't broken so they were broken for me. Yes, it was painful but it was the most amazing experience. At every stage of the pregnancy I thanked Jesus and my catch phrase became 'Thank you Jesus'. My baby is a miracle baby and although we gave him a biblical name, for short we call him TJ which is short for 'Thank you Jesus' and 'Total joy'. The name TJ for us is a reminder of what God has done and we also want it to serve as a reminder to TJ that he is no ordinary person but a living testimony.

The day that I came out of hospital was the same day that I received a letter from another hospital telling me that I could now receive IVF treatment. How ironic! I phoned the hospital and told them that I no longer required the treatment because I had just had a baby. The person on the other end of the phone asked me if I'd adopted a child so when I told her that I'd had a son by natural means, we both laughed together.

Through the whole experience my husband and I stood in faith believing in the word of God. My husband once told the consultant that he rejected what she was saying. She looked at him like he was crazy but my husband was confident and blatantly challenged the situation with the word of God. He stood on the truth which is the word of God. Now I truly understand the difference between truth and fact and for us the truth became a reality.

My son is now a year old and is walking and sucking his tongue and he loves to dance. He is my angel and sometimes I sit and look at him because I can't believe that I have had him. GOD IS LIFE and the bible says that his word does not return void. We used God's word and it came through for us. When we talk about faith the size of a mustard seed, I understand it to mean that God just needs something tiny to work with. The five percent gap that we had became a window and we stood on the word. My son is not mine, he belongs to God, and anyway he's too good looking to be our son so I know that he is God's baby who came straight from heaven! Hallelujah!

Chapter 13

Drugs

I started smoking pot at the age of eleven, but by the time I was four-teen, I was a heroin and crack cocaine user.

As the deer pants for the water brooks,
So pants my soul for You, O God.
My soul thirsts for God,
For the living God.

Psalm 42:1-2

I started smoking pot at the age of eleven, but by the time I was fourteen, I was a heroin and crack cocaine user. I always felt as if I was missing something in my life. As my mum brought me up as a single parent, I thought the thing that I was missing was a dad. At the age of fifteen, I received my first prison sentence and was sent to HMP Risley. The first few weeks were a complete shock, but then I easily got settled into the system.

I have wasted pretty much of my life by either being in jail or using drugs. I have been so unhappy that I have even tried to take my own life a few times. Each time I'd wake up a few days later in hospital and I'd question God as to why he did not take me. You see, I've lost three cousins; one aged twenty one who died of a heart attack, one aged seventeen who also died of a heart attack as heart disease runs in my family, and then another very close relative. She was sixteen when she was run over and I was with her and she died in my arms. Once again I asked God, 'Why not me?'

After that I started hitting the drugs hard and once again I ended up in prison. During my stay in prison I started to go to church and for once in my life things began to make sense. You see, now I believe everything happens for a reason. What the reason is I don't know. Maybe God never took me was because I had to find out what was missing in my life.

Now I know it was him and I can see a light at the end of my dark tunnel. Since childhood I have been trapped inside. At times I felt like I was going mad. I've heard people say that God speaks to them, but I've said my prayers and I've not yet heard him speak. But I'm at that stage where I want him to come into my heart to help me through things. I've got my whole life ahead of me now and I believe that one day he will speak to me. I pray that this day will be sooner rather than later.

Chapter 14

Death

I felt her heart and it was beating fast. I got her into the bathroom and she started getting weaker and weaker, then she fell and banged her head.

> *And it is appointed to men to die once,*
> *But after this the judgment*
>
> *Hebrews 9:27*

This chapter in my life that I am sharing is very sad because it's about the death of my mum. It all started in June 1999 when my mum began to put on a lot of weight. She went to the doctor and explained what was happening to her. They booked her an appointment for a check-up, which she was to attend three weeks later. She had her check up and after another two weeks, she was given her results, which at the time she was scared to look at. I was also afraid even though we both wanted to know what the problem was. I wanted to know what was happening to my best friend. Eventually I hugged my mum and opened her results. The letter said that she had been diagnosed with 'Cushions Disease' which is sometimes called 'Cushing's Syndrome' and was a condition which caused my mum's body to produce too much of the hormone Cortisol. The letter informed her that she would have to go to Christies Hospital in Manchester for one week to get her blood tested and to enable other checks to be carried out.

It was really hard for me to sleep that week, knowing that my mum was in hospital on her own, even though I visited her daily. Whilst in the hospital they carried out x-rays and various tests to find the best way to treat her. It was decided that she was to get a tube from her thigh through to her nostrils so that the disease could be withdrawn. After all of the tests, an appointment was made for her operation, which was to be on December 12th 1999. She was asked to be at Christies Hospital for 8pm that night. Early the following morning she had her blood tested and was moved to another local hospital. One hour later she was taken into the theatre where the procedure for the operation began. Surprisingly, the next day she was sent home, which neither of us was expecting. I asked her if she had questioned the doctors about it and she told me that they were the ones that had actually suggested that she be discharged.

During the week following her operation, my mum kept saying that she felt full and bloated like she was pregnant. I told her to phone the doctor and make an appointment as soon as possible. When she phoned the doctors, they told her that there were no appointments available until another week or more. She ended up not seeing the doctor. Day in and day out she felt the same. On December 28th at about 10.20pm, my grandmother phoned and talked with my mum for about half an hour. When she finished her conversation, my mum began to climb the stairs as she intended to brush her teeth before going off to bed. I walked behind her, as I normally would do. Suddenly she called my name and said that she felt weak. I helped her up the stairs. At the top of the landing she said to me, 'Feel my heart'. I felt it and it was beating fast. I got her into the bathroom and she started getting weaker and weaker, then she fell and banged her head. I asked my younger brother to watch over her whilst I called for an ambulance. I dialled 999 and told them through my tears what was happening. All I was doing was crying and I cried until I couldn't speak.

When the paramedics arrived, they would not let me near my mum. They told me that she was alright, even though I later found out that they had already told my aunt who had been called round, that she was dead. The ambulance took off and I followed behind in my aunt's car. After reaching the hospital I spoke to my mum, my best friend ever with tears flowing from my eyes. I let her know how I felt. I'll always love her. For me she will always be alive living inside of me and I hope that people can see her through me.

In my eyes this all happened because the medical services did not give her a proper check-up after the operation. During the process of the operation one of her blood vessels had burst which caused her to feel the way she did. She then developed a blood clot and died. This is a chapter in my life that I'll never forget and neither would I wish it on my worst enemy. It is not easy losing the one who brought you into the earth, especially when she's your best friend.

I had just turned sixteen years of age when my mum died. It is now 2007 and I am twenty-three years of age and my mum's death is a chapter in my life that will always remain with me. I'm in a new chapter of my life right now. The year after my mum's death, I spent the time doing very little. I began to move around with some new friends, partying and buying clothes every weekend. I was living life with my friends trying to be a hard person even though I was hurting on the inside. I broke up with my boyfriend and a couple of months later got involved in another relationship. I soon became pregnant; in fact I knew what I was doing even though emotionally I was not ready. But I gave birth to my child, my daughter, my beautiful princess. She filled part of the gap that I had in my heart. She will never be a replacement for my mum but through my daughter, I was given someone to love as much as I loved my mum, and someone to love me back.

As a child, I grew up in church and a seed had been planted, so one Sunday morning I got up and told my friend that I just had to go to church and give thanks for my daughter. I was told to expect difficulties at her birth but she was born safely and healthily, so I had much to thank God for. As I stood in the church, I began to give thanks and I became overjoyed and then convicted by God. I made a commitment to God and became a Christian. I recognised that God had helped me. He had a plan and a journey for me.

With God in my life I've kept myself and have not been in a relationship since. There is hope in loss and since I became a Christian God has used me to minister to people especially young people who are hurting. I can empathise and encourage and let them know that there is hope and that God is more than able. He can truly heal the broken hearted and set the captives free as he has helped me. I still miss my mum and feel the pain, but day by day I get strength and an inner peace to deal with my pain. At times when I am down God sends people who encourage me, or he gives me a scripture or even a song.

At times I ask the question 'Why?' My mum was my best friend and the only person that I could talk to. I also consider the 'What ifs?' Where would I be if that situation had not have happened? At times I can do nothing except just sit and cry over my mum, but I know that my redeemer lives. God knows why he allowed my mum to die that day. The gap will never be filled but through it all I am grateful to him because he has come into my life and the best thing that he did was to give me my beautiful daughter.

Chapter 15

Meningitis

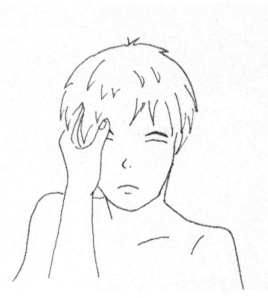

My body colour changed to a deathly grey. My family had given up on me because they thought that I was going to die.

I shall not die, but live
And declare the works of the Lord.

Psalm 118:17

Behold, a sower went out to sow.
And as he sowed, some seed fell by the wayside;
And the birds came and devoured them.
Some fell on stony places, where they did not have much earth;
And they immediately sprang up because they had no depth of earth.
But when the sun was up they were scorched,

And because they had no root they withered away.
And some fell among thorns,
and the thorns sprang up and choked them.
But others fell on good ground and yielded a crop;
Some a hundredfold, some sixty, some thirty.
He who has ears, let him hear!

Matthew 13:3-9

I was brought up in a Protestant family in a small village in Uganda. My father and mother used to go to church on an irregular basis, on occasional Sundays and sometimes at Christmas and Easter. They did not know God but only knew of the God of Sunday. When I was eight years of age, my dad died.

Three years later, I recall leaving primary school and walking home with one of my friends. I have been told that I fell down unconscious by the wayside. I was taken home and apparently began to fight with people and act like a crazy person. A strange language came out of my mouth which no one could understand. In my small village, there were no hospitals so my family had to wait until the next morning for a taxi to take me to the hospital in the nearby city. On arrival I was admitted in a state of unconsciousness and remained in the same state for one month. I could not eat or drink so was fed intravenously. This caused me to lose a great deal of weight. I also was unable to see, to walk or do anything.

My body colour changed to a deathly grey. My family had given up on me because they thought that I was going to die. Back at home in my village, they had even begun to prepare for my burial. The diagnosis for my sickness was meningitis. It was 1990 and this was a new illness in my country. For that reason there was no medication available to anyone, and most people who contracted it died from it. The few who survived became lame, crippled, paralysed or lost their sight.

One day, as I was lying still unconscious on the hospital bed, some 'born again' Christians came around praying for the sick. As a last resort, my mother called them over and asked them to pray for me.

They answered her request and came and prayed for me. The very next morning I woke up out of my coma. I felt like I had been in a very deep sleep and I had no idea where I was or what was going on. The first thing that I saw was the electric light above my bed. In my village we did not have electric lights so it was strange and surprising, even shocking. I could hear and I attempted to speak but for some reason, my mouth could not open. I tried to raise my head but my neck seemed to flop from side to side. It was unstable. I was asking myself questions. What had gone wrong and why was I here? I indicated to my mum through signs to get me some paper and a pen and even though I was very weak, I was able to write down the questions that were in my head. She began to explain to me what had happened and later told me about the people who the day before had prayed for me.

I began to improve and progress in my recovery. After three days, I began to speak again but my language was like that of a baby. Four days after that, which was one week after I had awoken, I was discharged from the hospital. I was still very weak and I remember that as we were walking back to my village, I had to be supported by others. Over time however I began to get stronger.

Once I had recovered, I questioned my mum as to the identity of the people who had prayed for me. She told me that they were 'born again' Christians so once I was fit and able, I went to look for them and on finding them I told them what had happened. Even though they had prayed for me, they were amazed at my recovery. A miracle had taken place in my life. They asked me if they could pray for me again. I accepted and I was happy for them to do so and as they prayed, I believed in the Lord Jesus Christ and became a Christian. Later my mum also believed as did the rest of my family.

Looking back, maybe it took my sickness to enable my family to be blessed. My whole village was also affected and benefited from the miracle in my life. Before I took ill we had no church in our village, now we have a church on my land and my mum is one of the elders and I too being one of the founders have a place in the ministry. I'm now a student at a Bible College in England and maybe when I return home I will plant churches to reach those people who were like my parents who visited church only occasionally and did not know God for themselves.

Chapter 16

Domestic Violence

I was beaten and dragged down the stairs and then he put a knife to my throat.

Finally, my brethren,
Be strong in the Lord and in the power of His might.
Put on the whole armour of God,
That you may be able to stand against the wiles of the devil.

Ephesians 6:10-11

Where I am now in life is a very peaceful and restful place. I believe that everything happens for a reason and everything that I have been through has helped me to be who I am today. Let me begin. I was in a relationship with a guy from school for about two years. When I found out that he was sleeping around with other women I decided to end it. I was hurt and it was a painful experience for me. About nine months after we parted and I met another guy. He was cute and we started to date. Going out with him helped me to get over the hurt of the previous relationship. It was at this time in my life that I was having problems at home and my relationship with my mother and step dad was breaking down. My new partner would usually visit me at my mum's home and he gave me the attention that I so desired and craved. There were days when he would phone me six or seven times. Deep down I honestly thought that the level of attention was weird, especially because we did not seem to go out that much, but I liked it and was not about to complain. Looking back I can see the signs but in the midst of it all I was blind.

At the time I was awash with so many emotions relating to my mum and our relationship. Sometimes I would go to sleep at my boyfriend's house to get away but one day after returning after three nights of sleeping out, I found that my stuff had been packed up and put into my sister's smaller bedroom. My bedroom was my space, my only closet yet I had been shifted out. I was devastated and angry so I decided to move out of my mum's home altogether and I moved into my boyfriend's place. Because of the breakdown of our relationship, I didn't see my mum for a while after that.

At first I didn't see an aggressive side to my partner. I do remember once that he grabbed me and his tone of voice was severe but I dismissed it and did not think anything further of it. Then he began to sell drugs and I heard that guys were after him. I also heard that he was seeing some else. Around this time, I had applied to go on the waiting list for a new house. I was dealing with so many emotions and could not deal with the fear of the police or other people coming to break down the door looking for him, so I decided to move to another city to be near to my grandmother. He wasn't happy and I know that he didn't like the idea of me moving out of Manchester. He became possessive and always wanted to know where I was. If I was late home he would get upset and I could see the aggressiveness and the controlling power he began to exert over me. Living with him was like living with my dad. Once when I was six months pregnant he punched me and I fell on the floor. I became very depressed, maybe it was the pressure of the baby but maybe at some time in the future things would change. My friends would tell me stories about him sleeping around with other women but I chose to ignore the tales; they were things that I did not want to hear. I made my mind up and moved out of Manchester for twelve months. My son was born but I continued to remain in the relationship and eventually I returned to Manchester after we found a house. We began to live together and this was the beginning of the most difficult period in my life.

At one stage during the relationship I went on holiday with my mum and other family members. Because of his possessiveness, my partner did not want me to go, but I stood my ground and joined them. It was a great feeling. He had wanted me to telephone him regularly so that he could keep a check on me, but out there I was far away and I felt free. I had time to think about changing my life. On my return, he picked me up from the coach station. The first thing that he did was to punch me in the face. It was a shock, but it was on that day that the realisation set in that I knew that I had to leave. When we finally arrived home he violently beat me. He had no reason to do this although I realise that it was his way of expressing his fear of what I might have been up to whilst on holiday. These were his insecurities and he was trying to instill fear in me so that I would never leave him. I felt trapped. As he questioned me, I knew that I had to leave the relationship but I had to be careful until I found the right time. I had to think twice about what I said, what I did or what I wore for fear of making things worse for me. It was a very dark period in my life. I would ask, 'Why me?' How could I get out of this, especially as he had threatened to kill me if I left him? Yet I was doomed if I stayed. There seemed to be no way out.

I began to ask God to give me the courage to get out. I prayed to God and he began to give me strength. There were times when my boyfriend would beat me and I could not feel it in my body. I knew that I had to get out because now he had begun to snap at his own son and I had begun to fear for his safety. I had to protect my son and I gained strength from knowing this. Throughout my pregnancy I had to deal with many emotions and I secretly blamed my boyfriend for my son's disability, maybe the cause had been his violence and the stress that he had inflicted upon me. I had been alienated by my mum and family who would not visit me and the only thing that kept me going was the love I had for my son.

There were many times during the relationship that I contemplated suicide. I needed to tell him that it was over and I needed to be able to tell him face to face. One day I picked up the courage and strength from somewhere to tell him. I knew immediately that I was going to get beaten up and this time he was to take it to the extreme. There was no attempt by my partner to hide the violence from my son which lasted that day for four hours. I was beaten and dragged down the stairs and then he put a knife to my throat. I felt that he intended to kill me, but somehow I knew that he would not succeed. I told him that I would stay, not because I meant it but because it was the wisest thing to do in that situation. I had to use my head. He believed me because he later went out and left me in the house. Maybe he thought that because of the state that I was in, I would not physically be able to do anything. He was wrong. I was able to summon the energy and will power from somewhere and I called a friend who came round and helped me to collect a few things and then I left for good.

Walking out was a relief but also very terrifying. I stayed with my friend for six weeks. I was unable to eat and I fell down to six stone in weight. My doctor said that my body had gone into a state of shock. During the latter part of our relationship I was studying beauty therapy at college and despite all of the violence, I successfully managed to graduate. There were times when fear grasped me and I would expect him to turn up at college but thankfully my fears never came to pass. It took at least twelve months for the fear within me to sub-side and through it all I had lost myself and become withdrawn. My self esteem had all but gone and even though over time I seemed to begin to come out, I was faking it. I was wearing a mask with all of the emotions, hurt and pain trapped inside of me.

After the completion of the beauty therapy course, I took on a coun-selling course. Often as students we would have to work in group sit-uations and at times I would be unable to speak and would sit silent-ly for up to two hours. It hurt me just to think about what I had been through. As part of the course we had to attend a retreat and we were told that we all had to participate. When it came to my turn no words came out of my mouth and instead I just burst into tears. This set the whole group off. I didn't say anything but it felt so painful however, the self development exercises that we had to participate in began to enable me to open up.

I was able to talk about how I felt rejected by my mum especially when she met my step dad. He used to beat us with belts and other instruments for no reason and he would usually do this when my mum was not around. This was something that I had never experienced before as a child as my dad had never ever beaten me. One day I felt that I had been through enough so I remember phoning my grand-mother and telling her. I found it much easier in the counselling ses-sions of the course to talk about my mother and stepfather rather than the domestic violence that I had experienced. I also found it difficult to talk about my son's disability. As well as studying counselling, I was also attending counselling sessions as I had been referred to these by my doctor. I'd also begun to attend a local church. I enjoyed going to church and my faith in God was growing. I specifically prayed and asked him to send me a male friend who would help me to overcome my fear of men and help me in the healing process. My prayer was answered and I bumped into an old school friend who was a member of the church. I knew that he was the one and he began to talk to me and help me to open up. I had begun to feel that men were all the same but when I met up with him I was able to talk about it.

The challenge for me today is to find out what it is that I am still holding onto. When I met my old school friend I had this fear inside of me that he would change once we got into a relationship. I know that this idea hurts my friend. This in turn hurts me, knowing that I am hurting him. At church I received Jesus as my Lord and Saviour and became a Christian and shortly afterwards I was baptised. During my baptismal service I was given an opportunity to share my testimony. I had fears of what people would think about my son's disability but in telling them I got a sense of freedom and also of healing. At this present moment I know that God is working in my life. I need to study the bible more so that I can grow spiritually although right now I feel like I'm at a standstill. I need to let go of the past but for some reason am afraid to do this, although I know that eventually it is going to happen. It is difficult to deal with all of the emotions within me but I know that God is a healer and I know that my future is no longer dark but is bright and through Christ I have a hope and a future.

Chapter 17

Suicide

Fear began to overtake me and a realisation that I was dying came over me, yet I knew that there was nothing that I could do.

> *My brethren, count it all joy when you fall into various trials,*
> *Knowing that the testing of your faith produces patience.*
> *But let patience have its perfect work,*
> *That you may be perfect and complete, lacking nothing.*
>
> *James 1:2-4*

Suicide was something that was on my mind for a long time. I can recall having an unhappy childhood and I was separated from my parents who lived abroad. I lived in London with guardians, and I was unhappy at the treatment given to me by those entrusted by my parents to look after me. At school I was bullied so thoughts of suicide would enter my head. I must admit that it started as a joke, but at times I felt that I really wanted to hang myself. I would self harm in places where it could not be seen, so for me suicide was not a matter of seeking attention but of leaving behind the hurt and pain.

It was whilst away from my parents that I was molested. I was fifteen years of age and it was Christmas. There was a group of us as children and young people staying together in a house that was absent of parents. We were all camping downstairs when a guy who was like a brother to me, began to try to feel my body and to kiss me. Yes, this was the start and it truly messed me up. I was confused by what had taken place, I was scared and I stopped eating because for some reason I believed that he would poison me. I had thoughts of suicide and at the time I attempted to take my own life by overdosing on my asthma inhalers. My attempt failed and everyone wanted to know my reasons for doing it. I told them what had happened but he denied everything, even turning things around by saying that what I was accusing him of was sick. He made me start to think that maybe I was the one who was sick. As children and young people, we agreed to resolve the matter by keeping it secret, not talking about it ever again and not telling our parents. The effect of this upon me was that I stopped talking about things that were bothering me and I stopped sharing my feelings. This caused problems in my family. For me talking seemed pointless as it felt as though no-one heard or understood. I think at the time, people probably thought that I was mad.

About a year later, I ended up having to go back to London and staying alone in the house where the molestation had occurred and being left alone with my molester. He tried to do it again to me but this time I was able to deal with it. We talked and he confessed and admitted that he had done wrong. It was quite a relief to hear the words come from his mouth. I told my sister but for some reason she told me that if it ever happened to me again it would be my fault. Her words stuck with me.

I was affected badly by the molestation. My sibling was the closest person to me and I felt that she and others were blaming me. I had so much venom against myself. It must have been my fault. In fact there was a time when my molester fell ill and I secretly believed that it must have been me who had indirectly caused his illness because of the venomous thoughts that I had within me towards him. I became very distant from my family and I began a rebellious phrase of my life. Sometime later I went out with a guy, slept with him and became pregnant. I was so cold and it was nothing for me to get rid of the baby. In fact the baby was not like a person to me. To me the thing inside of me was half me and half him. I was bitter and angry and did not want anything of his so the easiest thing for me was to abort it. I told a friend what had happened and she came along to the clinic with me, but this time I did not tell my family. After that it was hard for me to speak to anyone as I knew they would tell the others in our family circle and it would be a big discussion.

Before I aborted the baby I went to see a close friend of the family. It was his birthday and as we were talking, he decided to use me as a birthday present. He raped me. At the time that it was happening all I could think was that it was my fault. Thoughts of the past filled my mind as I tried to push him off, but I was not strong enough. The absurd thing was that his mum was downstairs during the whole assault. Afterwards I decided not to think about it or tell my family because as I saw it, nothing got done the first time around so why would things be different now? This molestation left me in a weird situation as the person is someone that I have to interact with even today as though nothing has ever happened. Until putting my story to print, I have never told anyone about this particular incident in my life. I don't talk to him about it, yet if I ever see him on the street, he starts texting me from his phone reminding me of his birthday. This whole chapter left me thinking sick and bad things of myself.

Sometime later I got involved with another guy who led me on a downward spiral. He had a warped mind and because of the vulnerable state that I was in, he was able to mess with my mind. He hated white people and believed that Jesus and Christianity was a religion devised by white men. Instead he talked of ancient gods and Egyptology. He started telling me about myself, analysing things that I did. I began to think that he could read my mind. He was a very disturbed young man and he had attempted to commit suicide a few times himself. I began to follow his beliefs and even wanted to paint my bedroom black. I know that I scared my family and they would not allow me to do this although we eventually compromised and agreed that I could paint the furniture black. I also painted a sinister mural on my wall. I had become a racist and although the mural was meant to signify 'Black Power', it was very disturbing to look at. When I was out with my boyfriend, he would sometimes communicate with me by drawing pictures of us together in a cage. He would tell me that we needed to get out; that we were trapped in the world and that the only way out was through death. I began to believe that what he was saying was the truth and that death was the way out of this world. It was a very dark period in my life especially as everything including college seemed to be going wrong for me.

One day I began to phone around those people who I was upset or angry with to try to talk and to ultimately make things better. The sad thing was that I could not get hold of any of the people that I felt I needed to speak to. I had wanted to talk to them to get them to understand what was wrong and why I was the way that I was. I had begun to feel that it would be easier for my family if I wasn't around anymore. It seemed to me that I couldn't change anything or anyone so the only alternative was for me to escape. These were the thoughts that had penetrated my mind on that particular day when everything came to a head. I was alone in the house and suicide had entered my thoughts. When I found that I was unable to get hold of the people that I had tried to call, I remember thinking of something that my boyfriend had told me and that was to take plenty of pills if you really wanted to escape. I therefore made a concoction from whatever pills I could get hold of that were in the house. I began to swallow them, washing them down with alcohol and water. Yet inside I felt guilty at what I was doing so to appease myself I began to phone people to at least say goodbye. I began to experience different sensations within my body and I felt weird. My first thoughts were that the feelings were good but as time went by I knew that I was losing control of my feelings and with that I began to get scared. Fear began to overtake me and a realisation that I was dying came over me, yet I knew that there was nothing that I could do. The feelings of guilt would not leave me. How would my mum and my family feel? What would this do to them? What about those people who had done me wrong?

From here on everything was a blur. Apparently I began to write, although I have no recollection of this. One of the friends that I had called had realised that something was wrong and had called an ambulance which arrived at my home. When the paramedics broke in, they found me in a state of semi consciousness. Because I had drunk so much I was vomiting and mumbling. I was rushed to hospital where I fully cooperated. It was a terrible experience having to swallow a tube and have my stomach pumped. Emotionally I felt bad. My family and friends were at the hospital and they were angry at me. They could not understand why I had not spoken to them about the way that I was feeling. I didn't want them to blame themselves. However, these feelings of remorse only lasted a short time before my thought pattern reverted back to its old ways. I wanted people to understand why I did what I did yet I still did not want to live. The doctor had a patronising attitude towards me and asked me if I would do it again. To appease him I told him I wouldn't. I was asked if I was trying to gain attention by my attempted suicide and again I gave him the answer that I thought he wanted to hear which was 'Yes'. Yet in the back of my mind I had begun to plot how I could do it again, but this time successfully. I didn't want to do the pill thing again and would definitely drink less. Maybe I could slash my wrist!

No-one talked about what I had done so I just physically shut off from the world. My mind was like this for a long time, I purposely closed it off. I sometimes lived in a bubble and would not talk for up to two days straight, even though I went through the motions of life. I remained like this for a long time. Whenever I was being normal, it was because I felt guilty. An appointment was made for me to go to the doctors who referred me to someone who I think was a psychiatric nurse. It was a pointless exercise because the whole idea was to talk, yet those closest to me had in the past told me to keep quiet. For this reason I would sit there during the sessions and not say a word. I've no idea what she must have thought of me.

I would have good days but I was always only waiting for the right moment, however I never tried suicide again to the same extent. After that I found that I couldn't look at myself in the mirror. One day I decided to face the fear and I sat in front of a long mirror. As I looked at myself at times my vision would become blurred and it was as though there was something else present. I ended up smashing the mirror and in this act I got my release.

A day came when I was forced into talking to my mum and this helped me in my healing process. I talked to her about everything including the molestation and the abortion. Her reaction shocked me. She was so calm and she spoke softly to me. I thought that she would be angry with me especially at the thought of her daughter being sexually active, but she was unruffled and good about it. This conversation helped me and it also changed and strengthened the relationship that I had with her. She realised that I was no longer a child, yet this change in our relationship also increased the guilt within me and I knew that if I killed myself, I would be hurting my mother.

I wasn't a Christian throughout all of this time. Now I am and have made a commitment to live for Christ. Nonetheless, even as a Christian, thoughts of suicide have not necessarily gone away. What has changed is that the level of guilt that I feel having these thoughts far outweighs the thoughts of suicide. It is a continuous battle. I had developed a skill of making people think that I was okay, telling them what they wanted to hear. However I am now a mother with a young child. For his sake I try to think positive thoughts and my son is my reason to live. I have to ask the question that if I were to kill myself, what effect would it have on him? I can't do that to him.

Looking back at the events surrounding the molestation and the rape, I realised that despite the fact that I was a victim, at the time I blamed myself. I believed that it was my fault. At the time that it was happening to me it seemed that those closest to me, my family and friends, reinforced this view. But looking back I know that they too were young like me and were expressing their opinions from a position of limited knowledge and experience. I don't put any blame on my friends or family as they were only trying to help me. I also no longer blame myself and I know that it was not my fault.

Before I became a Christian I can honestly say that I was not scared of death but I was afraid of the process of dying. Death was the place that I wanted to reach; it was my goal so I had to find out what would be the quickest way to achieve that goal. In becoming a Christian I actually became afraid of death, knowing that the outcome of my suicide would be to escape this life but to be destined for hell and destined for a place that is worse than this life here on earth. My concept of hell at the time was that it was here on earth and that we were living it now. I was wrong and now I have a different way of thinking and I know the truth. I realise that I am here for a reason and that there is a purpose to my life. I've learnt that it is sometimes impossible to change people or circumstances but I can change me and the way that I handle them. I manage and deal with situations and I make a way to feel better in myself by praying. By praying to God I know that I don't have to take it all, that there is a way out and that any problem can be resolved. The eyes of my understanding have been enlightened and this gives me a hope and a future.

Chapter 18

Cancer - Life

Up to that point I was okay but then it dawned on me that in a round-about way I had just been told that I had cancer, I had cancer!

I can do all things through Christ who strengthens me.
Philippians 4:13

It was 1996 and it all started with a dream. I am a person who regu-larly dreams and on this particular occasion I dreamt that there was a spider living under my armpit. Even though it was a strange dream and it recurred each night for one week, I ignored it. However, the last time that I had the dream I recall that I dreamt that not only was I telling people about the spider under my armpit, but at the same time I dreamt that I was showing them the spider whilst pulling out its wiggling legs.

The next day, I saw my cousin and told her about the dream and she asked me what I intended to do about it. I knew that I needed to act upon it so that day I went straight down to the local hospital's Accident and Emergency department and told them that I wanted to be checked out. They considered that I was not an emergency case and instead told me to go to see my doctor. I did as I was instructed and I visited my doctor. The reaction that I got was not the one that I expected to hear. I was told not to be so silly and questioned as to why I had gone to the A & E department in the first place. My doctor told me that it was nothing and I was turned away.

But the dream was becoming so real. Within two weeks of me first having the dream, my close friend's dad had died and whilst I was grieving with her, I developed a cyst under my arm. I went straight back to the A & E department telling them that I had been a few weeks prior. This time they did not dismiss me totally but gave me a letter to give to my doctor. When I went to see him he told me not to worry and referred me to the Nightingale Centre which is a specialist hospital department. I had to wait a week for my appointment but early one morning during the week whilst at home, I heard an audible voice call me by my name say, 'Do this'. I instantly touched my left breast. I remember looking around to see if my daughter was awake and had spoken as the voice sounded so real, but she was still sleeping. It was then that I felt a lump.

On the day of the appointment, I went to the Nightingale Centre and they carried out a needle test on the lump and told me to return in a week's time for the results. Whilst I was waiting for the results I continued to dream of the spider. I didn't tell anyone that I had been to the hospital even though I had told them about the dream. On my return, the doctors told me that they were concerned with the results and said that they wanted to repeat the tests. I sat there in silence as they looked at me. I said, 'What do you want me to say? Should I be asking loads of questions?' The doctor said that he knew I had been given some worrying news. Immediately I started to tell him about my dream. I think that I must have been in a state of shock at the news. I told the doctor that I planned to go to Africa for a holiday the following week. 'Would I still be able to go whilst waiting for the results?' The doctor's response was that it would be fine for me to go as I would only be away for a week.

When I had completed the second test and the consultation, I headed for the car park and sat in my car. Up to that point I was okay but then it dawned on me that in a roundabout way I had just been told that I had cancer, I had cancer! I sat in the car and bawled and bawled. There was no one else there except me and God. Then I picked myself up knowing that I had to drive home and I looked in the mirror and said, 'Pull yourself together.' I did just that. I went straight to the betting shop where I knew I would find my dad. He reacted calmly to the news and he told me that I would be okay. Next I went to see my auntie who lived close by. I was sweating when I arrived and when I told her that I had cancer she put her hands on her head and screamed 'Jesus!' I only stayed with her for about five minutes, and then I went to a friend's home and stayed there for a bit. Finally I went home and told my daughter that I was having tests but I could not tell her what the tests were for.

I took the holiday to Africa and during the whole week that I was there, I did not once think about the news that I had received. However once I was on the plane to fly home, my thoughts began to turn to what was to come. I arrived back in the country on the Friday and by the following Monday I was in hospital being operated upon. After the operation I had a consultation with the surgeon. I was told that it would be necessary for me to have chemotherapy and radiotherapy as the cancer was three to four centimetres in size and had grown since I had first been tested. Apparently the cyst that I had developed under my arm was a reaction to the cancer in my body.

During the operation, they removed seventeen lymph nodes of which one was found to be cancerous. It seems that the cancer had travelled around my body and returned to the point from where it had started. Because of this I was told that the cancer could have deposited anywhere around my body so this was the reason for the need for both chemotherapy and radiotherapy. The consultant said that I would need to consider the fact that there was a sixty per cent chance of the cancer recurring and returning within five years. To me this was the same as saying that I had a forty per cent chance of survival.

My dad and step mum came to the consultation with me. My daughter knew that I had a lump but I still had not told her what it was. The doctor went through all of the information and said that it was a big decision that I would need to make so I was to go home and think about it. It was a Friday and I remember just before I was going to bed I spoke to God. I knew that I needed to make a decision about my treatment, but I didn't know what the right decision was, so I was leaving it up to him. The following morning I distinctly heard a voice call me by name and say, 'Don't worry about the treatment, go ahead with it and leave your hair to me!' That was it, my decision was made and I was referred to Christies Hospital in Manchester for my treatment.

The radiotherapy should have been the worse of the two treatments for me but instead, it was the chemotherapy of which I was to have six courses on a fortnightly basis. Chemotherapy drugs are injected into the body but the nursing staff struggled to find my veins. To solve this problem they put something called a 'central line' into my body, through which they could inject the drugs. I called it my 'chemo line'. There were problems with my white blood cells which affected my immune system. I also had problems with the central line inserted into my body so I had to attend the hospital on a weekly basis and the chemotherapy sessions had to be done three weekly instead of fortnightly. In fact I was only able to have four of the six scheduled rounds of chemotherapy because it made me so ill. There were also many side effects and I remember a most traumatic occasion happening three days after my first treatment. I was having a bath when I noticed that all of my bodily hair had come out. Another side effect of the treatment was the feeling of itchiness. One day I asked my daughter and my partner to scratch me and I remember as they did this to my head, my hair began to fall out. Because of the effects to my body I was called in for a consultation meeting and was told by a professor that they would have to stop the treatment. I was told though that it was likely that the treatment had probably been successful.

Throughout it all the thing that stuck with me the most was the fact that I was told that it was likely that the cancer would return within five years. It affected the way that I lived so that even if I suffered the slightest headache, I would believe that it was the cancer that had returned. As far as I was concerned, I only had five years left so I decided to do all of the things that I wanted to do including spending six months in Jamaica with my grandmother who had raised me. I also went on a fantastic two week Caribbean cruise. During this five year period, I made sure that nothing was a problem to me. Things that I would have worried about previously, no longer bothered me. I was able to reflect on life and even though things were still going on around me, I began to put things into perspective. I read more and the Oprah Winfrey show was my daily tonic. During that time I changed my diet, consuming natural and pure foods which I could eat and drink to balance and complement the medications that the hospital had given to me. If I felt unwell at any time, I would just lie down and rest. I took things more slowly and when I went back to work, I went on a part time basis at first. I became a spur of the moment person, living for the moment rather than planning for the future.

I wasn't silent about what had happened to me. I went on holiday to New York and returned with a lot of books about cancer to give me a greater understanding of the illness. I would talk about it to friends and family who came to visit me at home although those closest to me including my dad, auntie and mum found it difficult to talk about it. It was something that had happened to me and I was glad that it had happened to me and not to my daughter or anyone close to me. My daughter seemed to outwardly show little response to what had happened to me but now I know it must have affected her deeply as she began to get into trouble at school. She otherwise seemed to be her normal self but I know that through it all she has been hurt deeply by me and the cancer. I remember once in a fit of anger when I was trying to deal with my own emotions, telling her and my partner that it was their fault that I had got cancer. Those are words that I said in the heat of the moment, words that were not true but they were words that I can never take back. My daughter's response was to become a qualified Social Worker so she could help people with problems. Also, no-one in our family has ever been known to have this type of cancer and because I was diagnosed with it at such a young age, the doctors have said that my daughter would have to be tested when she is thirty.

Before I was diagnosed with cancer I had always gone to church and would also send my daughter. In fact you could say that I was happy and comfortable with God and with my life. When I was ill if I was able or not in hospital, I continued to go to church. One Saturday, when my partner who had been a tower of strength to me throughout my treatments, came to visit me, I asked him if he would go to church the following day and ask the church to sing the song, 'I Surrender All'. After he left that day, I remember thinking about the words of the song that I had given to him. In my heart I knew that I had surrendered all, however my lifestyle did not reflect it. It was then that I decided to truly surrender all to God.

It is now eleven years since I had the cancer and I am glad that it happened to me as I don't think I would have reached where I am today whether mentally, physically or spiritually. I believe that it was something that I had to go through and I have been empowered by it and it has caused me to work on me. Before the cancer, I was busy doing this and that and I had no time for me. Once I got over the five year hurdle I was able to move into a more relaxed mode. I stopped living my life as though time was ending and have been able to use the tools that I have acquired.

In considering the past, I know that what has brought me through is the belief that I can do all things with the help of Christ. I believe that if I focus on something long enough with the help of Christ, it will come to pass. Throughout my life I have been told so many negative things but I've learnt not to focus on negative things instead only on positive things. No-one knows the cause of cancer or has yet found a cure. My thinking is that if I continue to do the same things that I was doing before I got the cancer, the chances are I will get the same result.

That is why I have a changed thought pattern. Now negative things are easier for me to shut out and stress does not have a lasting impact. I've learned to forgive and move on rather than hold on to my emotions and pain. Before, I was carrying so much unforgiveness, now if someone upsets me I forgive and I move on. I don't forget but I've learned to externalise the feelings rather than internalise them as I used to. In respect of my body, I have also changed my diet and am now a vegetarian eating a healthy diet. I realise that my body was filled with toxins through the cancer treatment and I'm not going to add more to them by eating meat.

God has done some wonderful things for me; he has changed me so that I am freer. In the last ten years he's taught me to speak out more and now I speak freely especially about the cancer. It is just one of those things which have happened. I believe that I am now cured and that when I die it will be because of something else. For me it was my 'wake up' call. For some, their 'wake up' call might be getting sent to prison, or a tragic accident, but for me, mine was cancer.

It was something that I had to go through - a process. It was my process which has drawn me closer to God and made me realise that there is no way that I could return to my former lifestyle. I can say that there is a God because I have proven him. It was God who told me to feel for the lump and to go through the treatment whilst he promised to take care of me. There is something out there bigger than the cancer, the doctor, the consultant and the surgeon and for me this is God who has given me the strength to survive cancer and all other adversities life continues to throw at me.

There is a song that we sing that I have found to be so true for my life. It says,

He knows my name,
He knows my every thought,
He sees each tear that falls
And hears me when I call.[1]

Be Blessed!

Chapter 19

Restoration

It was considered that I needed to be detained for my own health and safety as well as for the protection of other people.

If My people who are called by My name
Will humble themselves,
And pray and seek My face,
And turn from their wicked ways,
Then I will hear from heaven,
And will forgive their sin and heal their land.

2 Chronicles 7:14

It was spring 2004, I was at the end of two years of study at a Bible School in Europe and I had just returned to my home in England. During my studies, I had developed a deeper relationship with God through the study of the word of God. I had also been very active and had travelled to Israel and had recently completed a short term mission trip to India. For some unknown reason, on my return I began to feel desperately low and down in myself. I regularly used to pray to God and read the Bible so I couldn't understand this feeling inside. I was in a relationship and engaged to be married so this should have been an exciting time in my life, but deep down I knew that the relationship was not right so I ended it.

I was deeply troubled by the way that I felt so I went to see my pastor and shared with him how I was feeling. He prayed for me but as he did so, I began to shake my head uncontrollably and I started to groan. He immediately began to say, 'In the name of Jesus' and when he did this, I felt something moving in the back of my head. An assistant pastor was called and together they prayed for me. When they had finished they told me to go home as everything would be okay. But deep down, I still felt low and I knew that something was wrong. When I went to church that Sunday, I became paranoid thinking that people were looking at me. Pastor called me to the front and asked people to pray for me and as they were praying again I felt something inside of me. During the prayer I became so desperate that I even began to scream out to the brethren to help me.

A week later whilst I was in the bathroom getting ready to go to church, I heard an audible voice which said, 'Faith without works is dead and you're dead. You are accountable for what you know'. I knew it was the voice of the devil. After that I began to isolate myself and I knew that something was drastically wrong. Often I would sit at home and watch Christian television. One particular day I was watching the preacher Benny Hinn. At the end of his broadcast he always prays so as he was praying, I put one hand on the television and the other on my head. As I did, I felt something moving inside of me.

I was in a desperate state and people would come to my home to pray for me. When I was alone I would growl but no one knew of this. At other times I would be panting so heavily as though something was ripping my chest open. My skin was jumpy and would move and it became very itchy. My mum began to think that the cause must have been some sort of presence in my bedroom so she got some people to come and pray in my room. I became overtly paranoid and began to avoid people and not receive telephone calls. I isolated myself in my bedroom. In fact it got to the point where my mum who said that we needed to sort it out once and for all, asked me if I wanted her to take me to hospital. I knew it was something that she did not want to do and it was somewhere that I did not want to go. At the time I even had some Christian counselling but I was too scared to talk about what was going on so I did not mention the voices that I was hearing or the growling. I needed deliverance.

By Christmas 2004, my mum was truly stressed out and I overheard her talking to my grandad saying that she was going to take me to hospital. I was petrified but as I sat in my room, I just felt spaced out like something was gripping my head. I remember walking to the local post office and growling. Then I heard a voice telling me to kill my mum and her partner. 'If you don't you're dead!' The voice was telling me to do it and I was scared of not obeying it for fear of what it might do to me. When I came home I actually went forward to strangle her but stunned, she shouted at me and asked me what I was doing. It was then that I was admitted to hospital and during the admittance process I became violent and aggressive, even threatening rape. I was given medication which I refused to take orally so it had to be forcefully injected. In one incident five people had to hold me down and in another incident of violence the police had to be called. I was held under Section 3 of the Mental Health Act which allowed me to be detained in hospital for treatment. It was considered that I needed to be detained for my own health and safety as well as for the protection of other people. Under the conditions of Section 3, I could not leave the grounds of the hospital and so it felt like I was being held in a prison environment. At around this time my mum became a

Christian and even though I was in hospital she came to realise that what I was exhibiting was not of the physical realm but the spiritual. I had a spiritual problem that could only be resolved by spiritual means.

The scriptures tell us that God never leaves us nor forsakes us and despite being in hospital, God was working in my life. I came to meet another patient who helped me through. It was as though our meeting and the crossing of our paths was a divine appointment. I believe he had a discerning spirit. When I arrived I was kicking and growling and he just said, 'In the name of Jesus.' He asked me if I was okay and then told me that I was hearing voices in my head and feeling things in my body. He was right, up to this point I had not revealed to anyone that I was hearing voices because I was afraid of what might happen to me. I knew that God was using him to say things. He told me that the devil was attacking me to take me out. I began to hang around him and over time he began to get me to speak positive things. Also he told me not to resist the medication as the medical staff did not understand what I was experiencing.

I remember one day whilst in hospital having hallucinations and seeing the face of a demon on the wall opposite me. Next to him was a picture of me and I was crying out. I saw a pit with people in torment trying to crawl out, and Satan was with them. I began to shout out that Satan had my soul. The hospital staff came running in and I kept telling them to look, couldn't they see it? But there was nothing to see. I picked up the bible and cried to them that they needed to know that it was real. In reality, I felt that I was lost but they didn't have to face the same fate as me, they didn't have to experience hell.

During my time in hospital God was dealing with me and I realised that I was also suffering from psychological problems which stemmed from my childhood. These related to my father who when I was a child, would make promises to me but would always let me down. Because of the lack of attention from him, I had sought it in my fiancée but that was a wrong relationship. Whilst still in hospital, my friend got me to watch the film 'Liar Liar' featuring Jim Carey. As I was watching it I began to associate myself with the son in the film who was always being let down by his dad. I could see myself in the boy whose dad was always failing to keep his promises. The man in the film was my dad and I was the son. This realisation opened a door through which God began a healing process. Another time as I was playing a board game of chess it suddenly became a game for my life. It was as though I was playing a game against darkness, a game against the enemy of my soul and every move was a fight for my life. It was a game that I ultimately won!

I began to listen to taped messages by Christian preachers and on one occasion listened to one by Creflo Dollar. In his message he began to pray and it seemed like the power of God was on him and he was saying, 'Be free.' As I listened I began to pray and ask God for freedom. As I did I could feel the power of God all over my body. In my quiet times God began to speak to me about my purpose in life. He sustained me and looked out for me and my family. For example, whilst I was in hospital my grandad passed away. The fact that I wasn't able to be there really cut me up but even though I was on a Section 3, God granted me favour so that I was allowed out for the day of the funeral. My mum was also baptised whilst I was in hospital, God was truly working in my family.

But even though God was doing a work on me, I still needed some further spiritual intervention and I needed to be delivered from Satan's power over my life; there was something within me that needed to be cast out. I would spend time each day in the hospital chapel as it was the one place that I could feel safe and where I was able to pray. My mum obtained permission for a pastor and another of my friends to visit me and use the chapel. The pastor was a man of faith and filled with the confidence of God the first thing he said to me on his arrival was that I was going to be delivered that day. He was so clear, he truly believed it. We went to the chapel and as he began to cast out spirits I started to growl and crawl on the floor. I confessed to and repented of things that I had done in the past and I began to feel better. But even though I knew evil spirits had come out of me, it still felt as though there was something still there, the work was almost but not totally complete.

My mum was persistent and sent for another deliverance minister. It was arranged that I would be allowed home for a couple of hours each day so whilst at home I was ministered to by this person. She would call out names of different spirits and then tell me to breathe. As I did I could feel the spirits come out of my body. Once the process of deliverance was complete and I was free, the deliverance minister then went on to pray for my family home. The whole process of my deliverance and my restoration took a long while. God revealed to me that there was a root cause to my problem. A perverse spirit had entered me whilst on my mission trip to India. I remember the incident well and the person from whom it was cast out of, but the strange thing is that I didn't even touch the person yet it still was able to come into me. The real problem though was that I had an open door through which the spirit could enter because even though I proclaimed Christ, my life was not right and I was doing and watching perverse things. On completion of my deliverance I felt so grateful to God.

I really had believed that I was going to hell. There was a time when a scripture became so real to me. It was Mark 6:36-37 which says, 'For what will it profit a man if he gains the whole world, and loses his soul?' You see during the time whilst I was in hospital, I was no longer sure that I was still a Christian and I believed and was convinced that I was going to hell. I remember hearing the scripture quoted and something jumped inside of me. I was going to hell and the devil had my soul! These thoughts tormented me deeply. Once when I was at a wedding, I cried as they began to sing the song, 'Going up yonder'. The people were rejoicing but I couldn't join in with them, you see in my mind I believed that I was going to hell. It got to the point when I thought to myself that if I was going to hell then I might as well start to live and do the things of the world, so I began to act in a worldly way but it never felt right.

Through the whole process, the message of the 'Footprints' poster became real to me because I knew that Jesus carried me through. In my deliverance God restored me and opened doors for me. I now teach at my local church and the gifts of knowledge and prophecy have been restored to me. I'm now due to travel to Russia on a short term mission trip, my first since my deliverance. I'm back at work, in fact I received so much favour from my employers who kept my job open for me for two years whilst I went to Bible College and also during all of the time of my illness. In respect of my health, it has been fully restored and I am no longer on any medication. In fact today I have been discharged from even the hospital's outreach and outpatients department so that I never have to experience another visit from anyone in relation to my period of hospitalisation. My illness was seen as a psychotic disorder and I was considered as someone who could become schizophrenic, but praise God the diagnosis of schizophrenia which could affect all aspects of my future life was never put on any of my files.

I now have a clear direction and a vision for my life. God reminds me of the things that I need to do. My eyes are opened to what God is doing especially towards Israel and I can see a bigger picture. Today I understand that God has appointed us all and chosen us to bear fruit and make disciples. Holiness is expected of all of us who are Christians and my character and integrity are of great importance. If I work at developing my character and at maintaining my integrity, it will mean that I will do what is right even when there is no one around. Truthfully, the devil still tempts me with things that I used to do and there is still a battle that goes on in my mind. However I am more aware of the warfare and I have no fear of it anymore. Praise God, all fear has gone, I have been delivered, I have been set free and I have been restored.

Chapter 20

Sexual Abuse

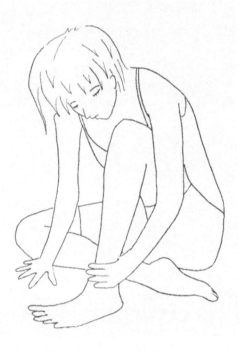

My cousin had a collection of pornography videos and magazines. He would show me a picture and try to imitate what he saw by performing sexual acts on me and the other children.

I will say of the Lord, 'He is my refuge and fortress;
My God, in Him I will trust.'

Psalm 91:2

I will praise You,
For I am fearfully and wonderfully made;
Marvellous are Your works
And that my soul knows very well.

Psalm 139:14

As a child my mum told me that the only reason that she did not abort me was because my dad was with her when she went to the doctors and found out that she was pregnant. Physical and emotional abuse from her was a standard part of life. She would hit and beat me in the head and face and would even smash things over my head. Once, my mum hit me over the head with a wine bottle until it smashed. The injury caused me to black out for a few moments. When I came round she looked at me. All I could see in her eyes was hate. There was no love there. She swore at me, told me to clean up the glass and then left. At the time I thought that I was going to die. I felt as though my mum despised me for being alive. Part of me did die that day.

I thought that physical and emotional abuse was normal behaviour as did I think that sexual abuse was normal. The sexual abuse was not from my mum but from a cousin of mine who used to look after us when my mum would go out with my auntie. It was whilst they went out together that he would abuse me along with my other cousins and even neighbouring kids who were left in his care. This abuse was not the type you read about in newspapers because it took the form of sexual abuse by children upon children. My cousin had a collection of pornography videos and magazines. He would show me a picture and try to imitate what he saw by performing sexual acts on me and the other children. We were forced to perform incestuous acts with each other then he would violate all of us. If we did not cooperate or cried, he would beat us. In fact we all endured his beatings because of our crying, including his younger brothers who were always crying.

As a child it was regular behaviour for us and we did not understand what was really happening. I had no concept of what was acceptable and unacceptable behaviour. Growing up into adulthood at one time I even found myself attracted to a close family member. It was disgusting but I knew that this was a result of what we were made to do as children.

As I grew up the circle of incest stopped but I continued to watch pornography and I would masturbate instead. I would baby-sit for my aunt and whilst the children were sleeping I would watch videos. This became normal practice and an addiction for me. I did not see anything wrong with it and I would play out on myself scenes from films that I had watched and things that I had seen in magazines. I had an imaginary world in my head which I would act out. In the most part I tended to stay away from relationships and looked after myself through masturbation. However, there were times when I was promiscuous and I remember that whenever I would have sex, I would cry throughout the whole process. I would find myself masturbating mostly when I was upset or lonely but even if I was in a relationship I would do it. I would even masturbate in college and no one would know what I was doing. Part of it was a desire for the physical touch on my body which as a child I received but as an adult was not getting.

As well as masturbation, I began to self harm using sharp objects. I would also hit myself with objects in the head. I may have targeted my head because that is where my mum would hit me. Also it was where the thoughts were and they were thoughts that I wanted to be rid of. I would self harm at the slightest thing, if I made a mistake or spilt, dropped or forgot something. Everyday things would trigger me off and I would blow them out of proportion. I would physically and verbally tear myself apart. If someone said something and did something and they were in the wrong, I would think it was my fault and I would punish myself for it. I would even self harm at college, getting upset if I could not understand or do my work.

At times it was as though I was on the outside looking in at myself. It was horrible and I thought I was losing my mind. During the act of masturbation it was like I was feeding something. When my mind entertained the thoughts it was as though spirits would take me to a place where I knew that I should not go to. I knew that it wasn't right but I couldn't stop. I would feel sick and after it was over I would cry or physically or verbally attack myself as a way of punishment. It didn't matter where I was, whether walking down the street in town or in church. I would hit myself in the head or dig my fingernails into my scalp, my arms or my legs. I felt hopeless, as if I was a useless waste of space and I wanted to die. I guess at one point I was hoping that if I hit myself in the head hard enough, I would knock myself out and not wake up.

I felt like I was going crazy and there were times when I wouldn't even go to church because I thought that God would reject me. I also thought that if someone looked at me they would be able to see right through me and see how dirty my mind was. The masturbation bothered me more than the self harm as in my opinion it was dirty and against God. I had no idea that the self harm was just as important an issue to him and that it hurt him each time I hit myself.

As a Christian I entered into an abusive relationship with a fellow Christian. At first he treated me well and I liked it, it was what I needed. We had become sexually active during the relationship and were fornicating but we decided to stop and were trying to live right. I still had a conscience and at times if he asked me to have sex with him and I refused, he would get upset and angry. As far as he was concerned, we'd had sex before so there was no reason for me to refuse. On one of these occasions he raped me. It was really strange because if anyone had walked in on us it may have seemed like we were having consensual sex. He was so strong but yet at the same time so gentle. It was as though he was in a trance. As soon as the rape ended I barricaded myself in my bedroom. Then he began to apologise and went into the kitchen, pulled out a knife and threatened to kill himself. I was the victim yet I was the one who had to convince him, the perpetrator, not to harm himself. I took the knife from him and as I went back into the bedroom and lay in my bed, I saw a dark hooded figure in the hallway. The air went very cold; I knew it was a demon. My heart thumped and I thought that I was going to die and that my boyfriend was going to come and strangle or stab me. The problem was that at no stage did I tell him to leave. It seemed that I had got used to people abusing me.

The next day he was unrepentant and turned around and told me that it was my fault because if I had fought harder or shouted louder then he would have stopped. At the time I had no self esteem left and I actually agreed with him. This man was insecure in himself and very possessive and this led him to becoming abusive towards me. I would do whatever he wanted me to do so that he would be pleased. He would make me feel guilty if I talked to another man or even looked at another man. One day I couldn't take the abuse anymore so I forced myself to have sex with him even though I knew it was wrong and not pleasing to God. I cried all the way through the act but it was my way of keeping the peace. I needed his approval, yet if we continued in this relationship we would be destined for hell.

The relationship finally ended, it had to end as it was destructive and it was ungodly. I left it hating myself. I felt worthless and I went downhill. I would masturbate and self harm, trying to find peace but unable to look to Jesus and ask him for help. I was very sad and at the time didn't dare tell anyone about the rape and I didn't report it to the police. I thought that they would judge me and say that it was my fault. Anyway, who would believe me? It must have been my fault because I chose not to leave. But I stayed with him because I believed that I could not survive without him. I assumed that I couldn't do any better and that I was lucky to be wanted by him.

Masturbation and self harm were subjects that I could not talk to anyone about. In fact I did once try to tell someone but later came to regret it. I knew that I needed help which is why I spoke to her. She and two other Christian women prayed with me but afterwards they went on to tell me that I shouldn't be doing it. They did not seem interested in the reasons why I was doing what I was doing and they made it sound so simple. I was close to admitting myself into psychiatric care as I was lost and felt that God had finished with me. There were times I thought about walking away from God. I thought that God could not help me, not because he was not all powerful but because it was me that was the problem; I had a defect. I felt like a total hypocrite who was sick in the head. People would look at me on the outside and would say how beautiful I looked yet they didn't know what was happening to me on the inside. They had no idea that I felt dirty. Once I decided to wear a hat to church. One woman commented about how nice I looked with a hat, in fact she said how 'saved' it made me look! I thought to myself that 'if only she knew'.

Life moves on and today I can say that I am a 'work in progress'. Four years ago I went to a Christian tent meeting where the preacher talked about a happily married woman who came to him for counselling as she was having affairs with men. She couldn't understand why she had done what she had done. In counselling her he asked her if she had ever been sexually abused and it turned out that she had been raped. The rape had opened a door in her life for a spirit of perversion to enter into her. That's when I understood what was going on with me. You see, my mind had buried the abuse that I had suffered as a child and I had forgotten it. To me I was just dirty and 'slack'. Until then, I had not been able to relate the way I was with the sexual abuse that occurred in my childhood. I started to go to counselling where I was able to talk about the abuse however my counsellor left so unfortunately the sessions to this day remain incomplete.

In respect of the masturbation and self harm, I have to work daily on my thoughts. If I were to continue on the same road, it would not help me but leave me in more pain. Now I know better and I choose to do better. I didn't wake up one morning and the desires had suddenly disappeared. No, it was and is a daily process. I had to understand the reasons why I did what I did and why I became who I was. Then I had to learn how to make the right choices. In the beginning it was a struggle as I still had the urges and would lose out each time, but the more I spoke to my urges using the word of God, the more it became easier to stop. Yes, it is a daily process and sometimes I still call myself negative things but I have to check myself and speak the word and use positive things. You see as a child and even in adulthood so many negative things were spoken over my life which I had begun to believe and speak to myself. Now I speak the word of God over my life to counteract all of the negative words that have been spoken. I still have natural urges but I know how do deal with them. I no longer feel guilty for them and I know how to make the right choices.

The more time I spend with God is the more I realise that he has done something in my life. I feel lighter. It is as though I was walking with heavy bags and someone came alongside me and without me knowing began to take the bags off me. The result is that the journey has become easier. I understand that the masturbation, self harm and low self esteem are the symptoms of the problem but that the root cause for me was the emotional and sexual abuse from my childhood. Truthfully, for a long time I have not been able to talk to God about the issue. I could talk to a counsellor who was physically present but have not always been able to speak to God because I felt dirty and unclean. For this reason the work is not yet complete but I know that I must speak to God and that as soon as I do I will be restored and made whole. I have now purposed in my heart to lay at God's feet the real issues, the emotional and sexual abuse that I have been through.

Final Word

Jesus said to him,
'I am the way, the truth, and the life.
No one comes to the Father
Except through Me.'

John 14:6

Every one of the men and women whose stories you have just read had two things in common. Firstly, they all endured some kind of suffering. Secondly, they all put their trust in the God of the Bible and allowed him to lead them through their adversity.

If you would like to have a relationship with God as the people in this book have, then why not pray this prayer. If you pray it with a sincere heart then Jesus will come into your heart and the door will be open to the Father.

Lord, I know that I am a sinner.
I repent and am sorry for my sin.
I believe that you Jesus died and rose to take away my sin.

Forgive me of my sin
I invite you Jesus into my heart
And accept you as my Lord and Saviour.
Lord fill me with your Holy Spirit.
Turn my life around and make a change.
Amen

If you have prayed this prayer or have been blessed by any of the testimonies that you have read in this book, please write to me at the address overleaf. I want to hear from you.

About the Author

Michelle Welch is an author, publisher and public speaker with a teaching ministry.

She lives in Manchester, northwest of England, UK.

She is a serving member of **Compassion Prison Ministries** and is also involved in various community based activities, missions and outreach work. She accepts invitation to speak.

Other publications
By the same author include:
The Mating Game (1999)
Real People Real Lives (2004)

Michelle Welch (Author)

If you would like to contact the author to let her know the effect that Real People Real Lives Volume Two has had on your life, or if you would like to purchase her other titles or for a public speaking engagement, write to:

Michelle Welch
Light News Publishing
PO Box 93, Manchester
M16 7BQ
England UK

www.lightnewspublishing.co.uk
e-mail: info@ligtnewspublishing.co.uk

135

NOTES